Hawaiian Anchialine Pools

🐚

Windows to a Hidden World

Mike N. Yamamoto
Thomas Y. Iwai Jr.
Annette W. Tagawa

Mutual Publishing

Copyright © 2015 by Mutual Publishing
No part of this book may be reproduced in any form or by any electronic or mechanical means, including information storage and retrieval devices or systems, without prior written permission from the publisher, except that brief passages may be quoted for reviews.
All rights reserved.

ISBN-13: 978-1939487-43-8
Library of Congress Catalog Card Number: 2014957329

All photos by the authors unless otherwise noted.
Background image on book cover © Alan Cressler
Design by Jane Gillespie

Second Printing, Feburary 2026

Mutual Publishing, LLC
1215 Center Street, Suite 210
Honolulu, Hawai'i 96816
Ph: (808) 732-1709
Fax: (808) 734-4094
email: info@mutualpublishing.com
www.mutualpublishing.com

Printed in the U.S.A.

In Memoriam

This book is dedicated to the memory of Isabella Abbott, John Bardach, Patrick Costales, J. Michael Fitzsimons, Takuji and Jean Fujimura, Kakkala Gopalakrishnan, James Izumi, Ronald Kama, Bert Kikkawa, Sherwood Maynard, Henry Okamoto, James Parrish, Richard Sixberry, Darrell Takaoka and Glenn Takeshita—beloved friends and colleagues whose friendship, wisdom and humor we will always cherish.

Contents

Mahalo Nui Loa!...vi
Foreword...viii
Introduction..xi

How Anchialine Pools are Formed...2
   What is an anchialine pool?...2
   Big Island..3
   Maui 5
   Oʻahu 7
   Molokaʻi 10
   Kahoʻolawe 11
   Kauaʻi 12

Biology of Anchialine Pools 15
   Eight Shrimp and a Crab 18
      ❶ *Halocaridina rubra*...19
      ❷ *Metabetaeus lohena* 26
      ❸ *Calliasmata pholidota* 31
      ❹ *Antecaridina lauensis* 33
      ❺ *Procaris hawaiana* 35
      ❻ *Palaemonella burnsi* 37
      ❼ *Vetericaris chaceorum* 40
      ❽ *Periclimenes pholeter* 43
      ❾ *Pele ramseyi*..45

Stream and Estuarine Transplants 49
  ❶ *Palaemon debilis* 50
  ❷ *Macrobrachium grandimanus* (juvenile) 52
  ❸ *Eleotris sandwicensis* 55

Nearshore and Tidepool Animals 57
Topminnows, Tilapia and a Prawn 61
Plants and Bacteria 65

Biogeography of Anchialine Pool Shrimp 68

Threats to Anchialine Pools 75
  Loss or Degradation of Habitat 76
  Introduction and Spread of Exotic Species 81
  Overharvesting for the Pet Trade 83

Habitat Restoration 85
  Big Island 85
  Maui 88
  Oʻahu 89

Biospheres and Micro-Habitats 96

References 101
Index 107
About the Authors 110

Mahalo Nui Loa!

This book would not have been possible without the support of many co-workers and colleagues.

Special thanks to Skippy Hau, the Division of Aquatic Resources' Maui Biologist and Matthew Ramsey formerly of the Division of Forestry and Wildlife for their invaluable assistance with surveys of anchialine pool habitat on Maui. Our Big Island staff, including Troy Sakihara and Troy Shimoda have provided and continue to provide data from the State's largest assemblage of anchialine pools along the Kona Coast; our Moloka'i Biologist, William Puleloa, for assisting with our surveys of the Kalaupapa peninsula and his kind words of support and encouragement written on the back cover; Lorena 'Tap' Wada and Aaron Nadig of the U.S. Fish and Wildlife Service have provided funding support, and assistance with surveys of anchialine pool habitat statewide; Dr. Charles Morgan of Planning Solutions made possible surveys of their anchialine pool restoration project at 'Ewa Marina; and Dr. Scott Santos and his staff at Auburn University, whose pioneering research efforts have contributed greatly to our understanding of the genetics and biogeography of anchialine pool organisms. Dr. Santos also kindly consented to writing the forward to this book.

Additional assistance have been provided by Tracy Tanaka, Alton Miyasaka, John Kahiapo, Tim Shindo, Lance Nishiura, Lorraine Takaoka, Glenn Higashi, JoAnne Kushima, Robert Nishimoto, Randy Honebrink and William Devick of the Division of Aquatic Resources; Joseph Fell-McDonald and Betsy Gagne of the Division of Forestry and Wildlife; Martha Yent of the Division of State Parks; William Aila, Chairperson of the Department of Land and Natural Resources; Chester Lao of the Honolulu Board of Water Supply; Joy Hiromasa Browning, Nancy Hoffman and Dan Polhemus of the U.S. Fish and Wildlife Service; Eric Brown of the U. S. National Park Service; Dr. Samuel Gon of The Nature Conservancy; Drs. Charles H. Fletcher III and Craig R. Glenn of the Department of Geology and Geophysics, University of Hawai'i; Dr. Sammy De Grave of the Oxford University Museum of Natural History; Dr. Charles H.J.M. Fransen of the Department of Marine Zoology, Naturalis Biodiversity Center,

Leiden, The Netherlands; Dr. Peter K. L. Ng of Raffles Museum of Biodiversity, National University of Singapore; Dr. Robert A. Kinzie III of the Department of Zoology, University of Hawai'i; Dr. John E. Randall and Arnold Suzumoto of the Bernice Pauahi Bishop Museum; Dr. David A. Weese, Georgia College and State University; Sherri Hiraoka of Townscape, Inc.; David Chai of the Four Seasons Resort at Hualālai; David Fukumoto of Fuku-Bonsai Cultural Center; Michael Furuya of 'Ōhi'a Productions; Alan Cressler for allowing us to use his beautiful anchialine pool photos; Robert Horii of the Honolulu Police Department and Bryan Yoshimura of Signs Plus & It's About Time.

Finally, we would like to recognize the contributions of a handful of scientists who pioneered the study of anchialine pools. L. B. Holthuis, the Dutch crustacean biologist was the first to describe these pools. Dr. Albert Banner and his wife Dora of the Department of Zoology at the University of Hawai'i discovered and described *Metabetaeus lohena*. Three other University of Hawai'i scientists: Dr. John Maciolek, formerly of the Hawai'i Cooperative Fishery Research Unit; Dr. Richard Brock of the Hawai'i Institute of Geophysics; and Dr. Julie Bailey-Brock of the Department of Zoology have been responsible for most of the landmark research on anchialine pools that followed. We are truly indebted to all of these individuals.

Financial Support for this publication, and the research that led to it, was provided in part by the State of Hawai'i, the Federal Aid in Sport Fish Restoration Program, and the State Wildlife Grant Program.

Foreword

Hawai'i Nō Ka 'Oi

The above saying, "Hawai'i (is) the best", might be heard as a reaction by first-time visitors and long-time residents alike to the beauty of the islands. Although true, Hawai'i is also "the best" and one-of-a-kind for other reasons as well. For example, many don't realize the Big Island is actually the largest mountain in our entire Solar System or forget the Hawaiian Islands is one of the only places on Earth where representatives of nearly every ecosystem can be found (where else can you play bundled up in frigid mountain snow and then snorkel in tropical waters of a coral reef in the same day WITHOUT getting on an airplane?). One of Hawai'i's lesser known, but truly spectacular, ecosystems is the topic of *Hawaiian Anchialine Pools*, habitats belonging to the anchialine ecosystem. As you will come to see, these land-locked ponds and pools containing freshwater to nearly full-strength seawater are most plentiful in the islands, come in a variety of shapes and sizes and are home to unique communities of plants and animals found nowhere else in Hawai'i or the world. The most common of these animals, the tiny shrimp 'ōpae 'ula and known to science as *Halocaridina rubra*, was one I caught and brought home as a keiki and am now fortunate enough to conduct research on as an adult. While others raised in Hawai'i may have also encountered 'ōpae 'ula in some context (these are the same shrimp you might find in decorative containers at your dentist's office, as wedding centerpieces or at various local stores), many likely don't know what they are, where they come from nor realized their natural habitats are being negatively altered or lost at an alarming rate. This book will serve these individuals well in developing a broader understanding and deeper appreciation for the habitats and organisms that comprise the anchialine ecosystem of the Hawaiian Islands.

Hawaiian Anchialine Pools collects and summarizes centuries of cultural knowledge as well as over 60 years of scientific research regarding the islands' anchialine ecosystem and the authors, Mike Yamamoto, Thomas Iwai Jr. and Annette Tagawa, have done an exceptional job with this daunting task. A particular highlight for me are the pictures of, and stories from, individuals who have worked in these habitats and with their organisms over the last ~10 years. Although relatively few in numbers, the dedication shown by this group of people should be readily apparent to the audience and has been truly amazing to be a part of. I think I speak for all of us in saying that we wouldn't consider what we have been doing as "work" in the traditional sense. Rather, its been more of a desire to satisfy our own innate curiosity into these remarkable organisms from an unusual ecosystem as well as to share this information towards educating those around us and preserving this dwindling natural resource. *Hawaiian Anchialine Pools* is one of these efforts and I sincerely hope that readers of all ages become just as fascinated and enchanted as we have been with the 'ōpae 'ula and the other organisms inhabiting the anchialine ponds and pools of the islands.

Enjoy the book and please remember: Hawai'i Nō Ka 'Oi.

Scott R. Santos, Ph.D.
Associate Professor
Department of Biological Sciences
Auburn University

Team members of the "'Ōpae 'Ula CSI Unit" of The Santos Lab at Auburn University in action at Cape Hanamanaioa, Maui, Hawai'i. From left to right: Dr. David Weese, Dr. Scott Santos and Dr. Justin Havird. *Photo by Matthew Ramsey.*

Introduction

Anchialine pool, Kapalaoa, North Kona District, Hawai'i. *Photo courtesy of Alan Cressler.*

Hawai'i has forever been blessed by a multitude of natural resources. Our forests, streams and nearshore waters are inhabited by hundreds of species of plants and animals, many found nowhere else on earth. Even in some seemingly barren areas along the shoreline, there exists a unique aquatic ecosystem underfoot. It is a subterranean realm of dark, water-filled caverns and crevices inhabited by rare shrimp, and other unusual aquatic animals. Anchialine pools provide us with a 'window' to this hidden world.

Anchialine pools occur worldwide, but the largest concentration of these pools can be found here in Hawai'i. They occur in a variety of forms, including: ancient limestone sinkholes on the 'Ewa Plain on O'ahu, a water-filled volcanic crater on the Kalaupapa peninsula on Moloka'i, a massive bomb crater on the Kaho'olawe shoreline, the gold and emerald green pools at 'Āhihi-Kīna'u on Maui, and a Kona coastline dotted with over 600 of the State's 700 anchialine pools on the Big Island. Hawaiian anchialine pools contain some of the rarest aquatic animals on the planet.

Introduction

Left: Authors Annette Tagawa and Thomas Iwai Jr., surveying an anchialine pool on O'ahu.
Right: DAR Maui Biologist Skippy Hau (in water) and author Thomas Iwai Jr. surveying an anchialine pool at 'Āhihi-Kīna'u, Maui.

Several years ago, we were shocked and disheartened to find one of the few sinkholes located on the Wai'anae Coast of O'ahu, filled with bags of garbage. Our hope at the time was that the individuals who did this were unaware that this was a unique and thriving ecosystem, and not just a hole in the ground. Perhaps the same could be said of fishermen who consider anchialine pools a convenient place to store baitfish for future fishing trips, or tourists who wade and swim in these pools. Our purpose in writing this book was to provide the layperson with a better understanding of how special and unique these pools are, and of the need to protect them for future generations.

There is an old scouting adage; take only photographs and leave only footprints—with anchialine pools, even footprints can cause lasting damage.

Lorena Wada of the U. S. Fish and Wildlife Service and Dr. Healani Chang of the UH Pacific Biosciences Research Center with students developing education programs dedicated to the cultural understanding and studies of anchialine pool ecology at the Kalaeloa Unit of the Pearl Harbor National Wildlife Refuge.

"O ka naʻauao o nā kūpuna ka lama
e hoʻomālamalama i ke ala no nā keiki."

"The wisdom of the elders is the torch
that enlightens the path of the children."

by Gary Kahahoʻomalu Kanada (1998)

How Anchialine Pools are Formed

What is an anchialine pool?

The term "anchialine" was first used by a Dutch crustacean biologist named L. B. Holthuis in 1973. The term comes from the Greek word 'anchialos', which means 'near the sea'. It was used to describe a unique type of brackish water pool found along the shoreline. Unlike tidepools, anchialine pools have no surface connection with the sea. Water, usually a mixture of seawater and freshwater runoff, enters the pool through subterranean cracks and fissures. These pools typically exhibit tidal fluctuations, with some pools becoming completely 'dry' on a low tide.

An anchialine pool is basically any natural, geological formation or man-made structure that reaches, or exposes the underlying water table. Some of the larger anchialine pools are simply depressions in lava fields, close to the sea. These pools can cover many acres and even provide habitat for water birds. Further inland, anchialine pools are typically smaller in surface area, but deeper in depth to reach the water table. All anchialine pools have two components: the part that you can see, which is referred to as the epigeal habitat, and the part that is underground, which is called the hypogeal habitat.

Diagram showing the epigeal and hypogeal components of an anchialine pool. *Illustration by Michael Furuya.*

Big Island

The Big Island contains about 650 of the approximately 700 anchialine pools found in Hawai'i. Most of these pools are located on the Kona Coast, between South Point and 'Anaeho'omalu. The best collection of pools is located in the Manukā Natural Area Reserve (NAR). These pools are the most pristine on the island and contain most of the rarer species of anchialine pool shrimp.

One of many anchialine pools found on the Big Island. *Photo by Troy Sakihara.*

On a wind-swept coastal plain, about a half mile northeast of South Point, is a unique anchialine pool called Lua O Palahemo. This is a large, water filled lava tube with a collapsed roof. This opening is about 30 feet in diameter, and reveals a pool of water approximately 60 feet deep. At the bottom of this pool is the lava tube itself, with one end of the tube extending 600 feet towards the sea, and the other end going about 300 feet mauka, towards the original source of the lava. Four species of anchialine pool shrimp: *Halocaridina rubra* (most commonly referred to as 'ōpae 'ula), *Procaris hawaiana, Calliasmata pholidota* and *Vetericaris chaceorum* have been found in Lua O Palahemo. Until it was recently discovered in a second anchialine pool

How Anchialine Pools are Formed

Aaron Nadig and Lorena Wada of the U. S. Fish and Wildlife Service prepare to survey Lua O Palahemo, Hawai'i for the rare anchialine pool shrimp, *Vetericaris chaceorum*.

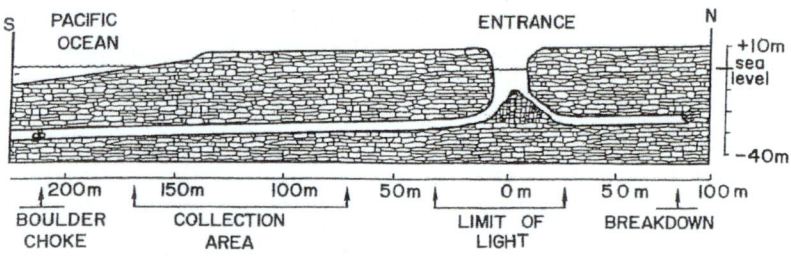

Cross-sectional drawing of Lua O Palahemo lava tube. *Illustration taken from Kensley and Williams 1986.*

in Manukā, this was the only place in the world where *V. chaceorum* was known to occur.

On the eastern side of the Big Island in the Puna district is a well-known anchialine pool that is a part of the Pohoiki Hot Springs. Located within Isaac Hale Beach Park, this small anchialine pool measures about 20 feet long by about 10 feet wide and was formed by a collapsed lava tube. The average depth is about four feet. The Hawaiian word 'Puna' means spring (of water) and percolating spring water can be found along the Puna Coast where cold spring water

How Anchialine Pools are Formed

Pohoiki Hot Springs, Hawai'i.

can be found bubbling up through the ground in several tidepools. At Pohoiki Hot Springs, underground volcanic activity heats up this spring water, which then mixes with the cooler seawater seeping into the pool from the ocean. The average temperature of this pool is about 98 degrees Fahrenheit, and the salinity is a low 6 parts per thousand (ppt).

Two species of anchialine pool shrimp: *Halocaridina rubra* and *Metabetaeus lohena* can be found in this anchialine pool. In a typical anchialine pool with these two species, the 'ōpae 'ula is normally more abundant. However, not only is Pohoiki unique because it is a natural hot spring, but the numbers of *Metabetaeus* appear to be higher than what would normally be seen in an anchialine pool with both species. Most of these shrimp can be observed crawling along the edges and walls of the pool, particularly in the warmer sections.

Maui

The largest concentration of anchialine pools on Maui is located in the 'Āhihi-Kīna'u Natural Area Reserve, on the southwest coast of Maui. This Reserve covers over 1200 acres, and includes the largest, and some of the most beautiful anchialine pools in the State. Many

How Anchialine Pools are Formed

'Āhihi-Kīna'u Natural Reserve Area, Maui, Hawai'i.

Wai'ānapanapa Cave, Maui, Hawai'i.

| How Anchialine Pools are Formed |

DAR Maui Biologist Skippy Hau and Dr. Scott Santos surveying Wai'ānapanapa Cave, Maui, Hawai'i.

consider 'Āhihi-Kīna'u the 'crown jewels' of the State's anchialine pool systems.

About 20 miles northeast of 'Āhihi-Kīna'u, on the road to Hāna is Wai'ānapanapa State Park. A key feature of the park is two water-filled caves, one of which contains 'ōpae 'ula. This anchialine pool is unique because of its low salinity (about 3 ppt.) and low water temperatures averaging 64 degrees Fahrenheit. This pool is also the one that is referred to in a well-known Hawaiian legend.

O'ahu

On O'ahu, which is much older than either Maui or the Big Island, the shoreline geology is very different. Instead of lava, much of O'ahu's shoreline is covered by ancient limestone reefs, which were formed hundreds of thousands of years ago when sea levels were much higher. As sea levels dropped due to vast quantities of water locked up as ice at the poles, these reefs were exposed. Rain and groundwater acidified by carbon dioxide in the atmosphere eroded this limestone reef creating fissures and caverns. These ancient, eroded limestone reefs are called karst, and it is within these formations that all of the anchialine pools on Oʻahu are found.

The porous nature of Oʻahu karst can be easily seen in some of the most famous structures in Honolulu. Kawaiahaʻo Church, ʻIolani Palace and ʻIolani Barracks are just a few of the historic buildings constructed of this material. The many cavities or 'pukas ' in the karst are clearly visible.

The ʻEwa plain is the largest karst formation on the island, and not surprisingly, contains most of the island's anchialine pools. These pools have also been found on the Waiʻanae Coast, on the North Shore, and Windward Oʻahu. Some of the pools are natural, while others are man-made. Most of the latter are wells, sumps, or other excavations dug into the water table for water quality monitoring purposes, or to withdraw brackish water for aquaculture purposes. Perhaps the most unusual anchialine 'pool' that we found was an 8-inch well shaft that had to be sampled with a custom made trap that was small enough to be lowered down the shaft.

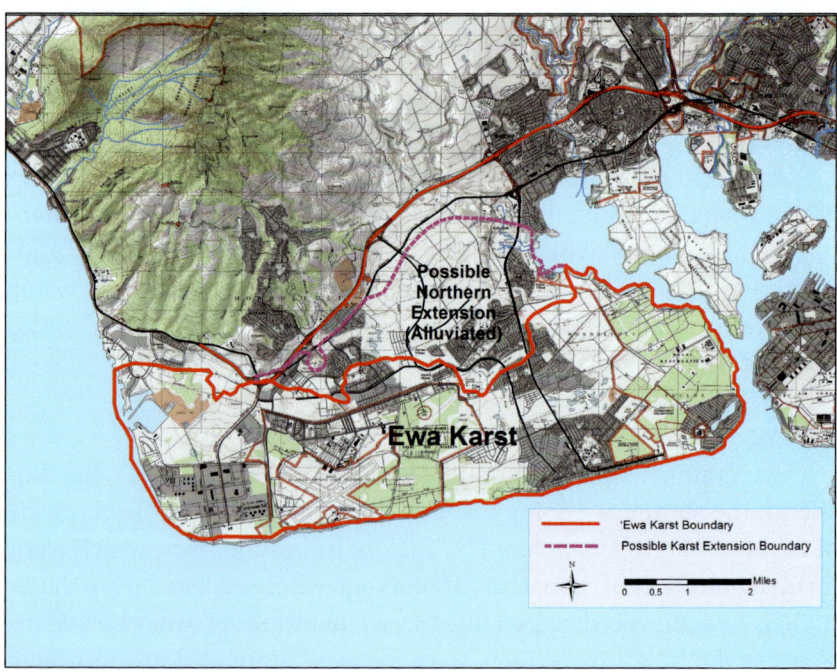

Location of Oʻahu's largest karst formation, the ʻEwa karst. *Illustration taken from Central Oʻahu Watershed Study, May 2007.*

How Anchialine Pools are Formed

Hidden entrance to a 12 feet deep sinkhole in Campbell Industrial Park on Oʻahu, Hawaiʻi.

Author Thomas Iwai Jr. photographing a small pool located at the bottom of the 12 feet deep sinkhole in Campbell Industrial Park, Oʻahu, Hawaiʻi.

How Anchialine Pools are Formed

Windward Oʻahu anchialine pool.

In general, Oʻahu anchialine pools are small, with most being just a few feet in diameter, and a foot or two deep. None of the pools discovered thus far possess the colorful cyanobacteria mats that many Maui and Big Island pools have.

Molokaʻi

In the middle of the Kalaupapa Peninsula, which juts out along Molokaʻi's north shore, is a large, water-filled volcanic crater called Kauhakō Crater Lake also known as Lake Kauhakō. Although this water body covers less than an acre, it is the 4th deepest lake in the United States. It is more than 800 feet deep, which gives it the distinction of having the largest depth to surface area ratio of any lake on earth. Surveys during the early 1970s revealed the lake to be highly stratified, with a brackish water layer several feet thick, floating on an 800 feet thick layer of salt-water. The saltwater layer was largely devoid of oxygen (anaerobic), but the brackish water layer was oxygenated and supported, among other aquatic life, ʻōpae ʻula.

How Anchialine Pools are Formed

Aerial photo of Lake Kauhakō, Kauhakō Crater, Molokaʻi, Hawaiʻi. *Photo courtesy of Eric Brown, National Park Service, U. S. Dept. of the Interior.*

At some point, and for reasons unknown, the stratification in this lake broke down. Sulfide rich saltwater, previously trapped at the bottom of the lake, rose to the surface releasing toxic hydrogen sulfide gas (rotten eggs odor). The previously habitable brackish water layer disappeared, and along with it, so did the ʻōpae ʻula.

Kahoʻolawe

In 1965, a series of tests were conducted to simulate the effects of a nuclear explosion on navy ships. Code-named Operation Sailor Hat, it consisted of a series of three explosions, each using a 500 ton charge of TNT detonated on the southwest shoreline of Kahoʻolawe. The resulting crater, called Sailors Hat, was about 75 yards in diameter and 15 feet deep.

In 1992, a biological survey of Sailors Hat was conducted by The Nature Conservancy, followed by a more comprehensive survey conducted by Drs. Richard and Julie-Bailey Brock in 1998. Both surveys reported the presence of small numbers of ʻōpae ʻula. In 2005, one of the authors (T. Iwai Jr.) had an opportunity to visit Kahoʻolawe, and surveyed Sailors Hat. The salinity of the water was 34.5 ppt, which was identical to the salinity recorded during previous surveys.

Operation Sailor Hat (1965). *Photo courtesy of the Naval History and Heritage Command, U. S. Dept. of Navy.*

The author deployed baited traps and lift nets, but surprisingly, was not able to collect any ʻōpae ʻula. A follow-up snorkeling survey along the perimeter of the crater confirmed the absence of ʻōpae ʻula.

The current absence of ʻōpae ʻula in Sailors Hat may be due to the presence of potential predators. A likely candidate might be an aquatic insect known as the water boatman (Family Corixidae), several of which were captured in the traps. Water boatmen are known to forage along the bottom and water column preying on small invertebrates.

Kauaʻi

The wet cave at Hāʻena certainly fits the description of an anchialine pool, yet anchialine pool shrimp have never been found here. In the past, Kauaʻi also supported a thriving aquaculture industry, which utilized wells tapping the brackish water aquifer. On Oʻahu, similar wells have revealed the presence of ʻōpae ʻula in the ground water. On Kauaʻi, this has not been the case.

How Anchialine Pools are Formed

Kahoʻolawe crater a.k.a. Sailors Hat, Kahoʻolawe, Hawaiʻi. *Photo courtesy of the Naval History and Heritage Command, U. S. Dept. of Navy.*

Kahuku well shaft where ʻōpae ʻula was observed on Oʻahu.

What could explain the absence of anchialine pool shrimp on Kauaʻi? One idea that seems plausible has to do with the geological age of Kauaʻi which has been estimated at 5.1 million years – making it the oldest of the main Hawaiian Islands. In older islands like Kauaʻi, there is less recharge of the ground water because water does not easily percolate into the highly weathered soils. On Kauaʻi, a higher percentage of the rainfall runs off into surface streams and then soaks into the ground. In the same fashion, karst formations along the shoreline may become less porous as they fill with sediment; to the point where they can no longer serve as habitat for anchialine pool shrimp.

Given the resilience of anchialine pool shrimp, it would not surprise us if isolated populations of these animals are discovered someday on Kauaʻi, or further up the Hawaiian chain. During the 1970s and 1980s, the Division of Aquatic Resources (DAR) was involved in the extensive surveys of the Northwestern Hawaiian Islands (NWHI) which is known today as the Papahānaumokuākea Marine National Monument. In hindsight, this would have been a great opportunity to also look for anchialine pools there. Subsequent studies have revealed that there is an anchialine pool located on Southeast Island of Pearl and Hermes Reef, but none of these mention any sightings of ʻōpae ʻula in the area. Hopefully, with greater awareness of these animals and their habitat, future expeditions to the NWHI will include at least a cursory search for anchialine pool habitats as part of their itinerary.

Biology of Anchialine Pools

Large numbers of 'ōpae 'ula in an anchialine pool on the Big Island. *Photo by Alan Cressler.*

As with the physical characteristics of anchialine pools, there is significant variation in the biology of these pools as well. Hundreds of species of plants and animals have been found in anchialine pools; ranging from microscopic algae to an extremely rare species of moray eel. The occurrence of these plants and animals in anchialine pools are dependent upon many factors, but two of the most important are: 1) the pool's connectivity to the sea, and; 2) the salinity of the pool.

Anchialine pools have no surface connection to the sea. The connections are underground, via cracks or crevices in the limestone or lava. If these subterranean openings are large enough, then fishes, invertebrates and algae typical of the adjacent shoreline can enter these anchialine pools, making them indistinguishable from nearby tidepools. The salinity in these pools is typically high (close to seawater), and there is little or no tidal dampening, which is the lag in the rise or fall of water levels in the pool with the tides. These

Dr. Scott Santos and Thomas Iwai Jr. sample 'ōpae 'ula in an anchialine pool located inland from the shoreline during high tide.

The same inland pool as pictured above is dry during low tide.

anchialine pools can be said to have a high degree of connectivity with the sea.

At the other end of the spectrum are anchialine pools that have a low connectivity with the sea. This could be caused by being located at farther distances from the sea and/or being formed in substrate

'Āhihi-Kīna'u anchialine pool located near the shoreline on Maui.

that restricts water flow. These pools typically display noticeable tidal dampening. Salinities are generally low and more dependent upon the amount of freshwater runoff present. The inhabitants of these pools can include various species of algae, amphipods and other small crustaceans, and perhaps salt-tolerant insect larvae.

The aquatic animals that are the focus of this book are found in anchialine pools that are somewhere between these two extremes. These pools have some connectivity with the sea, which allows the juveniles and larvae of these animals to move in and out of these anchialine pools, but not enough to allow the entry of predators. The salinity of these pools can be variable, with two species of shrimp: *Halocaridina rubra* and *Metabetaeus lohena*, occurring in both low and high salinity (more than 15 ppt.) pools. Five other species of anchialine pool shrimp: *Calliasmata pholidota*, *Procaris hawaiana*, *Palaemonella burnsi*, *Antecaridina lauensis* and *Vetericaris chaceorum*, are found only in high salinity pools. Two recent discoveries can also be added to this list: *Periclimenes pholeter*, a shrimp recently collected from an anchialine pool in Manukā on the Kona Coast, and *Pele ramseyi*, a newly described species of crab collected from pools in the 'Āhihi-Kīna'u NAR on Maui. Both of these species occur only in high salinity pools.

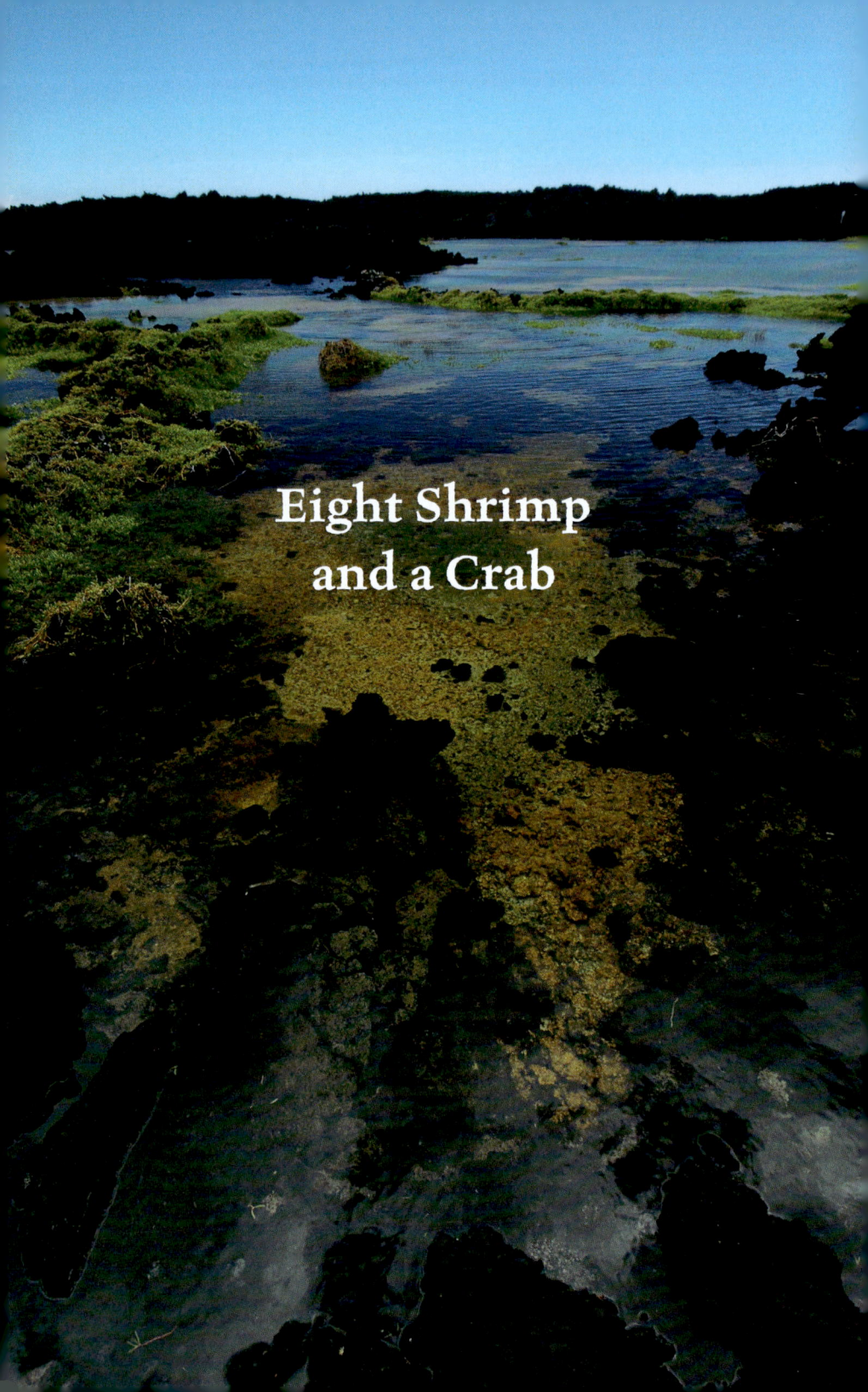
Eight Shrimp and a Crab

Eight Shrimp and a Crab

❶ *Halocaridina rubra*
ʻŌpae ʻula, ʻŌpae hiki

Description

This is the signature species of anchialine pools. Commonly known as ʻōpae ʻula, this tiny shrimp reaches a maximum length of about a half an inch.

Although the Hawaiian word 'ula' and latin word 'rubra' refer to the red color of this shrimp, they actually occur in a range of colors. On the Big Island and Maui, the predominant color is red. The color patterns of Oʻahu ʻōpae ʻula are more variable. Most are pink to clear, with some of the clear ones tinged with yellow or orange. At times, these pink and clear forms take on a banded appearance, with alternating red and clear body segments. A small percentage of Oʻahu ʻōpae ʻula are red, like those on Maui and the Big Island, or even white.

As with many animals, body coloration not only has a genetic component, but is affected by the environment and the animal's behavior (feeding, courtship, etc.). It has been speculated that the predominance of these clear and light colored ʻōpae ʻula on Oʻahu may be an adaptation to the light-colored limestone substrate in which

Biology of Anchialine Pools

'Ōpae 'ula size comparison. *Photo by David Fukumoto.*

'Ōpae 'ula color variations, white color variation with eggs along side the more common red variation.

Eight Shrimp and a Crab

'Ōpae 'ula red and white banded variation.

'Ōpae 'ula yellow variation.

'Ōpae 'ula, clear white variation.

O'ahu anchialine pools are found. By contrast, anchialine pools on the Big Island and Maui are found in dark, basaltic lava rock.

Distribution

'Ōpae 'ula are endemic to Hawai'i, that is, they are found only in Hawai'i and no where else in the world. Although they have previously been reported from Moloka'i and Kaho'olawe, to date, we have only been able to confirm their presence in anchialine pools on the Big Island, Maui and O'ahu. It was once believed that 'ōpae 'ula collected from Lua O Palahemo on the Big Island belonged to a different species, *Halocaridina palahemo*. Today, this is no longer believed to be the case, as they are now considered to be the same species.

Lifestyle

Diet: 'Ōpae 'ula are omnivorous. Although they feed primarily on algae, they will also feed on decaying animal matter, such as dead insects that occasionally fall into the pools. We also suspect that 'ōpae 'ula feed on the bacterial film that forms on rocks and other surfaces.

Reproduction: Like most crustaceans, the female 'ōpae 'ula carries her eggs under her tail. The eggs are about a millimeter in

Eight Shrimp and a Crab

'Ōpae 'ula, pink variation, berried female with eggs.

'Ōpae 'ula larvae in the process of hatching. *Photo by Bryan Yoshimura.*

'Ōpae 'ula larva.

diameter, and appear disproportionately large relative to the size of the shrimp. A typical clutch of eggs usually numbers less than twenty. After hatching, the larvae are born with a large yolk-sac reserve, which allows them to go through 12 stages before having to feed. This type of larval development is referred to as lecithotrophic. During this time, the larvae are considered planktonic, as it remains suspended in the water column, undergoing a series of morphological changes in the shape of its body and appendages. After about three weeks, the larvae settle to the bottom with their appendages becoming more specialized for filter feeding. By about the fifth week, the baby 'ōpae 'ula can be recognized as a post-larvae, or juveniles. It has the physical characteristics of an adult and begins its second mode of feeding by grazing on algae attached to the substrate.

Interestingly, gravid female 'ōpae 'ula and their larvae are normally not observed in anchialine pools. It has been speculated that gravid females seek the safety of their underground, or hypogeal environment to protect their eggs and newly-hatched larvae from potential predators. When maintained in tanks and micro-habitats, however, gravid female 'ōpae 'ula move freely about instead of remaining hidden. Similarly, larval 'ōpae 'ula born in captivity spend much of their time out in the open water. This difference in behavior between wild and captive 'ōpae 'ula is indeed curious.

Interesting Facts

As described earlier in this book, anchialine pools are the above ground, or epigeal habitat of these animals. It represents a small, albeit, important part of the habitat in which ʻōpae ʻula and other anchialine pool shrimp live. The subterranean, or hypogeal habitat is the dark, water filled crevices and caverns in the lava or limestone rock in which the anchialine pools are found.

We were curious to see if the ʻōpae ʻula could survive completely in the hypogeal habitat, and conducted a simple experiment in which ʻōpae ʻula were maintained in blacked-out and clear jars. Four one-gallon jars were filled with brackish water and limestone rubble. The outer surfaces of two jars were sprayed with black paint, while the other two jars were left unpainted. We randomly selected 40 ʻōpae ʻula and divided them into four groups. Each group was placed in a petri dish and photographed over a grid so they could be measured before being placed in the jars.

At the end of one year, the ʻōpae ʻula were counted and photographed again. The two groups kept in the dark jars had a 30% mortality rate, compared to a zero mortality rate for ʻōpae ʻula maintained in the clear jars. We also found that the ʻōpae ʻula from the dark jars were smaller in size. These results support the idea that while ʻōpae ʻula and other anchialine pool shrimp can live completely underground, anchialine pools provide these animals with a greatly enhanced food resource.

ʻŌpae ʻula have traditionally been used as bait to catch ʻōpelu *(Decapterus spp.)*. ʻŌpae ʻula were gathered and mixed with mud to form balls that would be used as palu (bait). A large circular net would be lowered between two canoes, and the balls of palu would be dropped into the net to attract the ʻōpelu. When the ʻōpelu gathered above the net to feed on the ʻōpae ʻula, the net would be raised.

For a tiny shrimp, ʻōpae ʻula are surprisingly long-lived. When properly maintained in captivity, they have been known to live from 10 to 20+ years.

❷ *Metabetaeus lohena*

Description

Like the ʻōpae ʻula, this shrimp is usually red in color, but can also occur in a number of color forms, such as orange, pink, clear and yellow. *Metabetaeus lohena* reaches about an inch in length, and is therefore about double the length of an ʻōpae ʻula. There is a large dark spot in the center of its head behind its eyes, which are tiny and black in color. They also possess a large pair of pincers. Another great distinguishing characteristic is the swimming motion of the *Metabetaeus,* or 'Metas' for short. Unlike the ʻōpae ʻula, Metas swim quite a bit faster, and have a smooth, gliding swimming movement. ʻŌpae ʻula will usually swim a short distance, stop and forage. So when viewing an anchialine pool from above, the larger red shrimp swimming rapidly along the bottom will probably be *Metabetaeus.*

Distribution

Metabetaeus lohena are indigenous to Hawaiʻi, which means that although they are native to Hawaiʻi, they can also be found elsewhere. In the case of *M. lohena,* populations of this shrimp have recently been discovered on Rapa Nui (Easter Island).

Metabetaeus lohena, red and pink variations.

Metabetaeus lohena, clear variation.

Lifestyle

Diet: It's been generally believed that *Metabetaeus lohena* is a predatory species that feeds primarily on the ʻōpae ʻula. Based on our

Biology of Anchialine Pools

Metabetaeus lohena pursuing 'ōpae 'ula.

Metabetaeus lohena, berried female.

observations, however, we feel that Metas are more properly described as being omnivorous. We've maintained these animals in aquaria set-up exactly like our 'ōpae 'ula tanks with just algae covered rocks. They appear to do well even without the addition of external food. *M. lohena* also seem to co-exist with 'ōpae 'ula, both in aquaria and

Eight Shrimp and a Crab

Metabetaeus lohena larva.

anchialine pools. Although we've observed them pursuing 'ōpae 'ula, we've never observed a Meta actually catching one. Our colleague, Dr. Scott Santos, has observed Metas in a Big Island anchialine pool voraciously feeding on caterpillars that fell into the pool from an overhanging branch. In addition, Dr. Richard Brock has observed *M. lohena* preying upon mosquito larvae in an aquarium setting.

Breeding: Unlike female 'ōpae 'ula, gravid female *Metabetaeus* can often be observed in anchialine pools. Female Metas carry about three dozen eggs, which they incubate in typical crustacean fashion under their tails. The incubation period is about a month. The newly hatched larvae, unlike the larvae of the 'ōpae 'ula, possess a small yolk sac. These planktotrophic larvae must feed to further develop. Microscopic examination of the larvae after the first molt revealed that one of its appendages (first pleopod) became modified into what can be described as a spear—extending up to four times its original length and terminating into a point. This spear-like appendage has also been observed in spiny and slipper lobster larvae, which utilized this appendage to immobilize their prey.

It's clear that *M. lohena* larvae must leave the anchialine pool complex and return to the sea to complete their development. Their larval development stage is probably longer than the 'ōpae 'ula's. Attempts to raise *Metabetaeus* larvae in captivity have thus far been unsuccessful.

Interesting Facts

This shrimp was first described in 1960 by Dr. Albert and Mrs. Dora Banner of the University of Hawai'i at Mānoa. The original specimens were collected from an anchialine pool located near an old cinder cone called Pu'u Lohena near South Point on the Big Island, hence the specific name 'lohena'. *Metabetaeus lohena* is related to the snapping shrimps found in marine waters.

Metabetaeus lohena.

❸ *Calliasmata pholidota*

Description
Calliasmata pholidota is one of the larger anchialine pool shrimp. It grows to more than an inch in length, and looks like a larger, more robust *Metabetaeus*. Like the Metas and the 'ōpae 'ula, this species can be found in a range of colors, from clear and red-orange, to an almost fluorescent pink. It also has pincers, which are quite noticeable.

Distribution
This species is indigenous to Hawai'i. It occurs in a few anchialine pools on Maui and the Big Island, and surprisingly, in an anchialine pool on the Sinai Peninsula, near the Red Sea.

Lifestyle
Diet: *Calliasmata* is probably omnivorous like *M. lohena*. One of the authors (M. Yamamoto) remembers watching two *Calliasmata* in a small, narrow anchialine pool on Maui. There were lots of 'ōpae 'ula in this pool, which would jump out of the path of the two *Calliasmata* as they barreled their way along the bottom of the pool. It was hard to decide if the *Calliasmata* were actually trying to catch the 'ōpae

Biology of Anchialine Pools

Calliasmata pholidota, red variation.

'ula because they seemed so clumsy and inept. These shrimp definitely have a good sense of smell, because dropping pellets of tropical fish food in the water will quickly get them to come out of hiding to forage.

Breeding: Nothing is known about their breeding habits, but based on their distribution pattern, their larvae must have an extended development phase.

Interesting Facts

As noted above, this shrimp has a very disjunct distribution pattern. Two other species of anchialine pool shrimp; *Metabetaeus lohena,* and *Antecaridina lauensis* share this distinction.

Calliasmata pholidota specimens at 'Āhihi-Kīna'u, Maui.

❹ *Antecaridina lauensis*

Description
This shrimp is light to dark red in coloration, with small white pincers and tiny white eyes. In the field this is a good way to distinguish them from ʻōpae ʻula, which have black eyes. They can grow to a little more than half an inch in length, which makes them appear like a slightly larger ʻōpae ʻula.

Distribution
This species is indigenous to Hawaiʻi. In addition to anchialine pools on the Big Island and Maui, *Antecaridina lauensis* has been found in Fiji, the Solomon Islands, Okinawa, Europa Island (west of Madagascar), and Entedebir Island (Red Sea).

Lifestyle
Diet: Like the ʻōpae ʻula, this species is omnivorous. They feed primarily on algae, but they will take advantage of other types of food that might become available. In an aquarium setting, for example, they will readily feed on tropical fish food.

Breeding: Nothing is known about their breeding habits, but since they are found in other locations far from Hawaiʻi, it is likely that they have an extended larval development phase.

Biology of Anchialine Pools

A pair of *Antecaridina lauensis* and one *Halocaridina rubra*.

Big Island anchialine pool with *Antecaridina lauensis*. *Photo by Troy Sakihara.*

Interesting Facts

As the photos illustrate, in captivity, 'ōpae 'ula apparently do not feel threatened by *Antecaridina lauensis* and will remain in close proximity to this shrimp. In the field, however, one or the other always seems to be dominate in pools in which they are both found, suggesting that they have different food or habitat preferences.

Eight Shrimp and a Crab

❺ *Procaris hawaiana*

Description
   This shrimp is pink to light red or orange in coloration, with a darker pink to red line that runs down the middle on the upper part of its body. The upper part of the carapace is often white to yellow in color. The eyes are small and black in color. *Procaris* lacks any obvious pincers or claws. The legs are instead covered with fine bristle–like setae. This shrimp is one of the larger species of anchialine pool shrimp, reaching a little more than an inch in length.

Distribution
   Procaris hawaiana is endemic to Hawai'i, and is found in only two pool groups on Maui, and two pools on the Big Island.

Lifestyle
   Diet: This species is a filter feeder, and seems to be constantly on the move. As it swims, it spreads its setae-covered legs to form a basket to filter and trap plankton and other tiny food particles. In captivity, it will trap and feed on live, newly-hatched brine shrimp swimming in the water column, and skim particles of fish food from the water's surface by swimming upside down just below the surface of the water. It has tiny

Biology of Anchialine Pools

Procaris hawaiana—note setae-covered appendages.

eyes for such an active shrimp, and seems to guide itself more by touch, using its antennae, which are spread widely as it swims about.

Breeding: Nothing is known about the breeding habits of this shrimp. The specimen in the photo on page 35 is a female. The eggs in her ovary are clearly visible through her carapace, and are orange in color.

Interesting Facts

This species was discovered in 1972 by Dr. John Maciolek, formerly with the Hawaiʻi Cooperative Fishery Research Unit at the University of Hawaiʻi at Mānoa. It is extremely rare, with only three known populations; two on the Big Island and one on Maui. It belongs to a primitive shrimp family called Procarididae. Only a handful of species are known, and all come from anchialine pool type habitats.

Procaris hawaiana eating its molt. *Photo by Troy Sakihara.*

❻ *Palaemonella burnsi*

Description
This shrimp is very different from the other species of anchialine pool shrimp described thus far. It is a small species ranging from 0.2 to 0.3 inches in size and has a transparent body liberally sprinkled with chromatophores. Perhaps the most noticeable feature of this shrimp is its pincers or chelae, which are long and slender. *Palaemonella burnsi* also has large, well-developed eyes. This suggests that this shrimp probably does not spend much time in the underground, or hypogeal environment, where such eyes are not needed, and in fact, would get in the way. All of the other anchialine pool shrimp have small, very poorly developed eyes, and are either blind, or visually impaired.

Distribution
This species is indigenous to Hawai'i, and has been found in anchialine pools on Maui and the Big Island. It has also been found on the inner reef flats in Okinawa Island, Ryuku, Japan indicating that this species is not limited to anchialine pool environments.

Palaemonella burnsi **about to ovulate.**

Lifestyle

Diet: This species is carnivorous and is a very efficient predator of the ʻōpae ʻula. It uses its large chelae to encircle the ʻōpae ʻula, and its smaller chelae to seize and dismember its prey. One of the authors (M. Yamamoto) observed this shrimp stalking an ʻōpae ʻula in a large aquaria and was amazed at how quickly the ʻōpae ʻula was caught.

Breeding: As you can see from the accompanying series of photos, female *P. burnsi* can carry quite a number of eggs. The eggs are mint green in color, and during the process of ovulation, move from the ovary within the carapace, to the swimmerets under the tail. This process takes just a few minutes. The incubation period is unknown, as is the amount of time it takes for the larvae to develop.

Interesting Facts

This species was named after John A. Burns, who served as the second governor of the State of Hawaiʻi. Governor Burns was instrumental in establishing the ʻĀhihi-Kīnaʻu Natural Area Reserve, preserving one of the State of Hawaiʻi's most impressive complex of anchialine pools.

Palaemonella burnsi in mid process of ovulation.

Palaemonella burnsi berried female.

Photo by Troy Sakihara.

❼ *Vetericaris chaceorum*

Description
This is the largest of the anchialine pool shrimp found in Hawai'i, reaching a maximum length of about two inches. It is yellowish orange in color.

Distribution
This shrimp is probably one of the rarest animals on the planet. It is endemic to the Big Island, and had previously been known from only a single pool complex—Lua O Palahemo near South Point. It has since been found in a second anchialine pool complex in Manukā. Its very limited distribution is one of the reasons this species was designated as endangered in 2013 under the Endangered Species Act.

Lifestyle
Diet: This species is known to feed on crustaceans. Captive specimens were observed feeding on 'ōpae 'ula, which were being kept in the same aquaria.
Breeding: Unknown

Interesting Facts

Like *Procaris hawaiana*, *Vetericaris* belongs to the family Procarididae, a very primitive group of shrimp. Both are very active swimmers. In 2010, Troy Sakihara, one of DAR's Big Island Biologists, observed and collected this species from an anchialine pool complex in Manukā. His personal account is presented below.

My first account of *Vetericaris chaceorum* at Manukā was during a series of diurnal/nocturnal anchialine biological surveys in March 2010. Towards the end of our study, I set out to collect specimens to photograph for our report, namely the anchialine shrimps. While collecting specimens, I came across a large, fast-swimming shrimp that I initially thought was an extremely large *Procaris hawaiana*. The shrimp continuously swam in a convoluted pattern through small crevices, under rocks, and momentarily throughout the water column, only to quickly disappear between the cracks again. Thinking that a large specimen would be perfect for photos, I was determined to catch it.

Armed with only a small, fine-meshed aquarium scoop net, I crouched anxiously at the pool's edge, waiting for the shrimp to reappear. Luckily, within a few minutes the shrimp suddenly swam out from a crack out of the corner of my eye. I quickly placed the net in front of the shrimp, and to my surprise, it swam right in. I took it back to camp to my makeshift photo studio, took a few shots of it, and then released it back into the pool none the wiser. It was only when I looked at my close-up photos of my prized '*P. hawaiana*' specimen back in the office that I realized I had something much more valuable and rare. I pulled up the paper describing *V. chaceorum* by Kensley and Williams (1986) and found that everything about my photographed specimen to be alike. However, because this species is so rare and had never been recorded outside of Lua O Palahemo, I asked for a second opinion about its identification from colleagues, one of which referred me to an expert on shrimp taxonomy.

Enter Dr. Sammy De Grave of Oxford University Museum of Natural History. After looking at the photos, Sammy agreed that it was likely a *Vetericaris*, but he needed a specimen to be positive. We then returned to Manukā a few weeks later and were fortunate enough to collect two specimens for him. Upon receiving the specimens, Sammy confirmed that it was of the genus *Vetericaris*, although some variation in morphometrics between our specimens and

DAR Big Island Biologist Troy Sakihara surveying an anchialine pool. *Photo by Troy Shimoda.*

the holotype from Lua O Palahemo raised some questions as to whether it was *V. chaceorum* or a new species. After thorough examinations by Sammy and his colleague, Dr. Charles Fransen, it was concluded that the Manukā specimens were indeed *V. chaceorum*, confirming for the first time a new record of this species outside of Lua O Palahemo. These findings were published in Crustaceana in 2013.

It is important to note, however, that we were not the first to document the presence of such a shrimp at Manukā. The late Dr. John Chan, formerly of the University of Hawai'i at Hilo, described a shrimp of similar size, color, shape and behavior in his 1995 report on nocturnal surveys conducted at Manukā. Our findings thus corroborate his observations of an unidentified shrimp, and confirm it as *V. chaceorum*. Further, John's observations prove that the established population of *V. chaceorum* at Manukā is not a recent occurrence.

Eight Shrimp and a Crab

Photo by Troy Sakihara.

⑧ *Periclimenes pholeter*

Description
This shrimp is pink to red in coloration with a number of red bands across the tail. It has two long pincers that are usually equal in size. Males can reach about 1.3 inches in length, with females growing slightly larger.

Distribution
This species is indigenous to Hawaiʻi. Thus far, it's been found in only two anchialine pools in Manukā on the Big Island. As with *Metabetaeus lohena, Calliasmata pholidota* and *Antecaridina lauensis,* this species has a very disjunct distribution pattern. It has been found in other areas of the Pacific, such as Fiji, New Caledonia, Sulawesi, Indonesia, and even the Red Sea and the Sinai Peninsula.

Lifestyle
Diet: Unknown
Breeding: Unknown

Interesting Facts

Until quite recently, this species was not reported from anchialine pools in Hawai'i. One of our Big Island Biologists, Troy Sakihara, was able to collect two specimens from a small complex of anchialine pools in Manukā in 2010. According to Troy, although *P. pholeter* is more abundant than *Vetericaris chaeceorum*, it was much more difficult to catch. They were very wary of foreign objects, such as nets or traps, and would quickly shy away from bright lights. These shrimp were also very quick, and capable of darting away in any direction, which made it difficult to anticipate the shrimp's movements and position the net accordingly. *Periclimenes pholeter* would also constantly crawl between rocks on the bottom of the pool, making it impossible to net them without snagging the net on the rocks. After many attempts, Troy was able to coax two specimens into a fine-mesh monofilament net.

The confirmation of the identity of the two specimens as *P. pholeter*, has significantly expanded the range of this species, which was previously limited to the Western and Central Indo-Pacific region. Amazingly, besides shallow water anchialine pools, these shrimp have also been found at depths of over 2,000 meters in the Red Sea.

Anchialine pool habitat for *Periclimenes pholeter*.
Photo by Troy Sakihara.

Photo by Matthew Ramsey.

❾ *Pele ramseyi*

Description
The carapace or body of this crab measures about 0.4 inches in width for adult males, and 0.5 inches in width for adult females, suggesting that the females are generally larger than the males. This crab is translucent with white to beige undertones in males, and orange to orange-red hues in females.

Distribution
Pele ramseyi has thus far been found in only three complexes of anchialine pools within the ʻĀhihi-Kīnaʻu Natural Area Reserve on Maui. The pools are within 20 meters of the shoreline and have salinities ranging from 30 to 33 ppt.

Lifestyle
Diet: Unknown

Breeding: Unknown, but the male and female specimens described above were caught on the same ledge in July 2010, which suggests possible breeding behavior.

Interesting Facts

This rare species of crab is the first reported to be found only in an anchialine pool environment. Although it has been previously observed by others, it eluded capture for decades. In July 2010, our friend and colleague, Matthew Ramsey collected a male and female specimen from an anchialine pool in 'Āhihi-Kīna'u. This crab not only represents a new species, but a new genus as well. The genus name *'Pele'*—the Goddess of Fire, honors its Hawaiian heritage, and the species name *'ramseyi'* will forever honor Matt. To his friends it will simply be known as Matt's crab.

The following is an account of Matt's efforts in collecting this crab taken from Dr. Peter Ng's 2011 paper in Zootaxa, describing Pele ramseyi:

> As for trapping the little critter, the crab is extremely difficult to catch. I've been trying for the last 5 years without success until last week. The only reason I was able to catch it was pure luck. Each crab was sitting on a ledge when I saw it, so I was able to put one net under the ledge and chase it over the ledge and into the net with another net. It has been extremely difficult to lure the crab into a trap of any kind. I've tried bottle traps and other traps of different shapes and sizes, equipped with a variety of baits, all without success.
>
> The difficulty lies in the shy behavior of the crab. If there's bait of any kind in the anchialine pool, the more aggressive species are usually the first to enter the traps. Larger *Grapsus* crabs are usually the first to charge in, as well as any *P. debilis* shrimp that might be around. Even if there are only anchialine shrimps in the pools with the crab, the crab won't go near the bait if *Calliasmata, Procaris* or *Metabetaeus* are near it. I've even made traps that had extremely thin entry holes, but caught nothing but ōpae ula or *Metabetaeus*.

Anchialine pool crab, *Pele ramseyi*. Photo by Matthew Ramsey.

Eight Shrimp and a Crab

Night survey at 'Āhihi-Kīna'u, Maui, Hawai'i. *Photo by Matthew Ramsey.*

The pools that the crabs are found in are shallow (1 to 2 meters at the deepest) with lava substrate. For most of the pools, there's no sand silt, or vegetative matter on the bottom. In one of the pools there is some algae, and a very small, thin patch of fine silt, but this location is the exception. The pools are close to the shoreline (approximately 20 meters) and the salinity ranges from 30 to 33 parts per thousand. Unlike some of the other pools, the pools with the crabs often have marine species, such as *Parhippolyte mistica,* and small, bright pink crabs that I've observed in tidepools along the shoreline.

I've observed these crabs during surveys conducted both during the day and night. Although I seem to remember seeing them more often during the night surveys, this may be due to the fact that they are more obvious at night due to the light color of their shells contrasting against the black rocks. I can definitely say that I have seen them only during times of high tides. I do not recall ever seeing them when the tide was low.

These crabs are usually found just at the edge of a crack or hole in the rocks. They usually sit facing outwards with their pinchers extended. At first I thought that this was to reach out and snap up some shrimps passing by, but I have not observed any actions like that. The only behavior that I have observed is one of defense or panic. When the large shrimp walk or swim by, the crab opens and extends its pinchers. Not surprisingly, it did this when I tried to corner it with a net. The usual reaction that occurs when it feels threatened is that it runs very fast. Since they usually position themselves next to a crack, it is easy for them to quickly disappear into the rocks.

When they are in the open or moving, they fold their pinchers against their bodies. I can't say whether they can see well or not, but it appears that they are at least sensitive to light and movement. They do not seem to notice me during the day if I sit quietly and observe them. If my shadow covers them, however, they will flee. The same thing happens at night if the beam from my flashlight falls on them for more than a second or two.

I tried to move extremely slow and slide my hand into the water of the pool, but as soon as the water starts to ripple, it seems that the crab can sense the motion. After seeing all the setae on the crab, it made me realize why the crabs were so sensitive to water movement.

The crabs are usually solitary with one or rarely two in a pool. If there were more than one in a pool, they were usually far apart. Other than the time that I was successful in collecting them, there was only one other occasion when I observed two crabs next to each other, but they quickly dispersed when I tried to collect them.

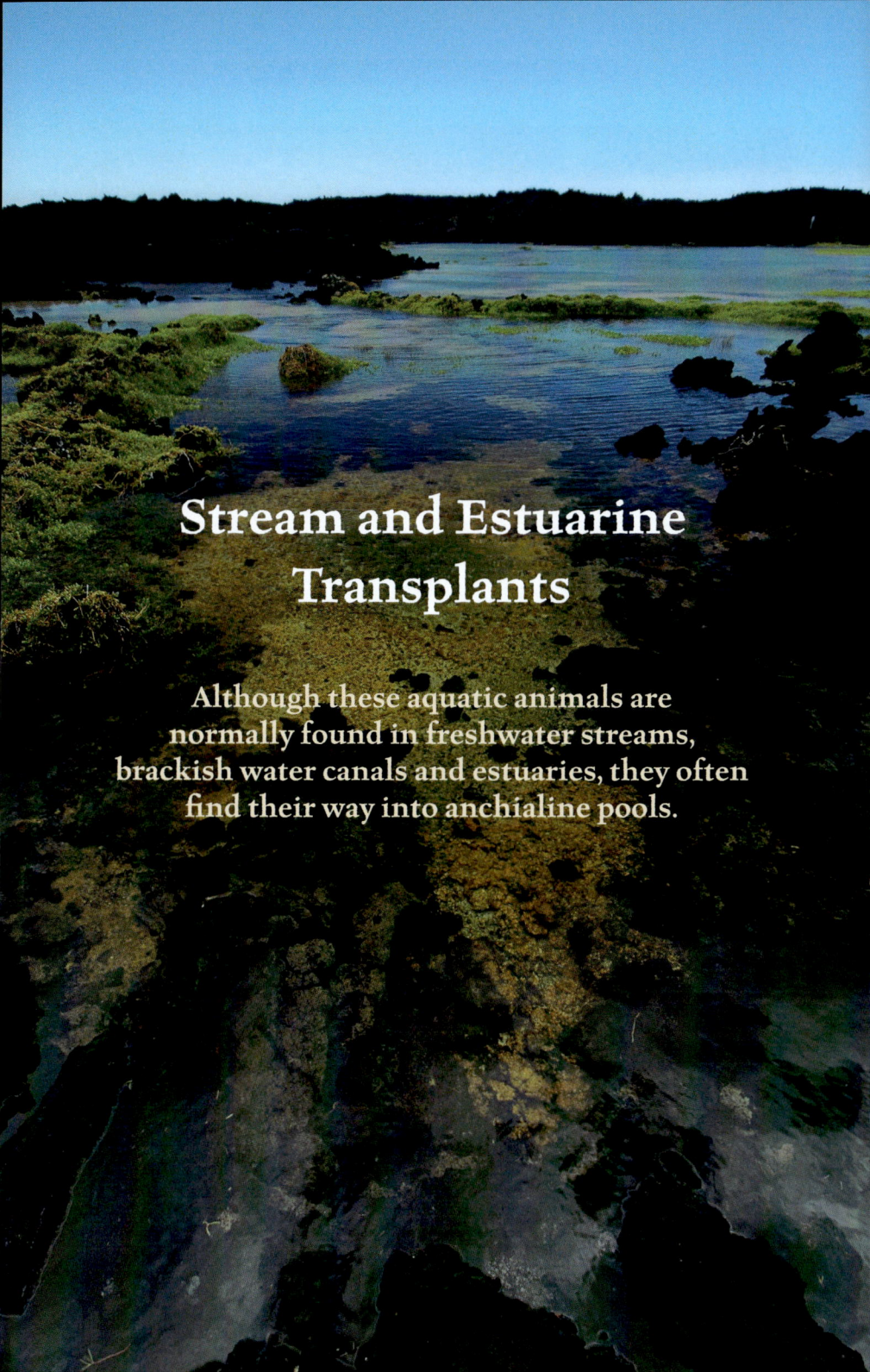

Stream and Estuarine Transplants

Although these aquatic animals are normally found in freshwater streams, brackish water canals and estuaries, they often find their way into anchialine pools.

❶ *Palaemon debilis*
ʻŌpae Huna

Description
The ʻōpae huna is a small estuarine shrimp, often found in anchialine pools. It grows to slightly more than an inch in length. It is transparent, and can be distinguished from other species of ʻōpae by a pattern of white spots and black lines as well as blotches on its body and tail. The rostrum, which is the spike between its eyes, is long and curves upwards. The eyes are large and bulbous.

Distribution
This shrimp is indigenous to Hawaiʻi, and is also found throughout the Indo-Pacific. It is typically found along protected shoreline areas, in brackish water canals and stream estuaries.

Lifestyle
Diet: This ʻōpae is omnivorous, feeding on a variety of plant and animal matter.

Breeding: Like most shrimp, the female carries her eggs under her tail, attached to her swimmerets. The incubation period for the

Stream and Estuarine Transplants

'Ōpae huna, *Palaemon debilis*, in a pool on O'ahu.

eggs and length of time it takes for the larvae to develop into postlarvae are unknown.

Interesting Facts

This small 'ōpae is a favorite bait of nearshore fishermen. It is used to catch many shoreline fishes, such as 'oama, āholehole and pāpio. Throughout the Territorial days of the earlier 1950s, dock pole-fishing was a favorite pastime for local residents and a way of life for still many others. During these years the demand for 'ōpae huna for bait was so great that it was imported via Moloka'i and sold live by many mom & pop fishing supplies stores that once lined Honolulu Harbor. To keep the 'ōpae huna viable during transportation, they were gathered and simply packed in wooden boxes lined with dampened 'akulikuli-kai (*Batis maritima*). This cozy arrangement eventually came to an end with the changing of the times and the modernization of Honolulu Harbor which discouraged people from fishing off the docks.

During aquatic surveys of anchialine pools along the Kona coastline in 1972-73, Drs. John Maciolek and Richard Brock found two different forms or ecotypes of the 'ōpae huna. They found the 'normal' form in clear water pools, and another form with an opaque body and short rostrum found in a pool with turbid water. The rostrum is the spike-like structure found between the eyes of crustaceans. The number of teeth found on the upper (dorsal) and lower (ventral) surface of the rostrum is sometimes useful in identifying the species.

❷ *Macrobrachium grandimanus (juvenile)*
'Ōpae 'Oeha'a

Description
Adult 'ōpae 'oeha'a can be easily identified by its dark brown coloration, and by the uneven size of its pincers, one being much larger than the other. The size disparity of the pincers may not be as obvious in very young specimens, but as the photo illustrates, the coloration of young 'ōpae 'oeha'a is very distinctive. It would be difficult to confuse juvenile 'ōpae 'oeha'a with either the 'ōpae huna or *Palaemonella burnsi*. The 'ōpae 'oeha'a can grow to about 3 inches in length.

Distribution
This shrimp is indigenous to Hawai'i and is also found on Okinawa Island, Ryuku, Japan. It is typically found in the lower reaches of streams, and can sometimes be found in anchialine pools.

Lifestyle

Diet: 'Ōpae 'oeha'a is omnivorous and feeds on a variety of plant and animal matter.

Breeding: The female carries her eggs under her tail until they hatch in about a month.

Interesting Facts

Considerable research was conducted at the State of Hawai'i's Ānuenue Fisheries Research Center in the 1960's on the closely-related Malaysian prawn, *Macrobrachium rosenbergi,* and the Tahitian prawn, *M. lar.* This research led to the development of a large aquaculture industry based on the Malaysian prawn. One of the authors (T. Iwai Jr.) played a major role in the development of this industry. One critical discovery was that although *Macrobrachium* are freshwater shrimp, their newly-hatched larvae are swept down the rivers and develop in the brackish and marine environment before returning to the stream after about a month as baby shrimp. This type of a life history is referred to as amphidromy, and is characteristic of all of our native stream animals.

Amphidromous animals like the *Macrobrachium* prawns and our native freshwater gobies typically have an extended larval development phase. Although fairly long, the 30 to 45 days that *Macrobrachium* larvae take to develop pales in comparison to the 4 to 6 months that native freshwater goby larvae are believed to spend in the ocean. This long larval development phase aids in the distribution of these animals over vast distances of ocean, and is what allowed these animals to colonize the Hawaiian Islands from other island groups in the Indo-Pacific. It also explains why these animals are sometimes found in anchialine pools.

After these animals complete their larval development and become post-larvae, they begin to seek freshwater to find a stream in which they can live. Unlike baby salmon, which will return to the same stream in which they were born, the young of amphidromous species will seek any freshwater source. One of the authors (M. Yamamoto) remembers setting up a temporary holding tank for some freshwater fish at the Ānuenue Fisheries Research Center on Sand Island, in Honolulu Harbor. It was a flow-through system with the excess water flowing out through a standpipe, which was supported by a piece of hollow tile. The trickle of freshwater flowed approximately 200' along a paved driveway, down a boat ramp, and into Honolulu Harbor. After about a week, while adjusting the tilt of the standpipe, he was amazed to find a dozen baby freshwater 'ōpae kalaʻole, *Atya bisulcata,* in the splash zone under the tile. The 'ōpae post larvae were apparently swimming in the harbor, picked up the trickle of freshwater flowing down the boat ramp, and followed it to the source.

With capabilities like these, it's not difficult imagining the baby 'ōpae and 'o'opu swimming along the shoreline and finding the freshwater seeps from anchialine pools. If the openings in the rocks are large enough for them to enter, they soon find themselves as residents of an anchialine pool rather than a freshwater stream. For freshwater 'o'opu, these pools are reproductive dead ends. The environmental cues that they require for spawning, such as freshets or high water flows are not present in anchialine pools. For the 'ōpae 'oeha'a, however, anchialine pools make perfectly suitable habitat. These 'ōpae are normally found in the lower sections of streams, often in brackish water estuaries.

During their 1972-73 Kona coast surveys, Maciolek and Brock also found two different ecotypes of the 'ōpae 'oeha'a in some anchialine pools. One form resembled the robust, heavily pigmented form normally found in freshwater streams, while a second form was more delicate in appearance, and not as heavily pigmented. This suggests that the 'ōpae 'oeha'a in at least some of these anchialine pools are reproducing, and some of the resulting larvae are returning to these pools possessing minute differences in their DNA which make them more adaptable to living in anchialine pools. Over time, this could result in the development of a new strain of 'ōpae 'oeha'a that will be different enough from the 'ōpae 'oeha'a normally found in streams to be considered a new species.

Stream and Estuarine Transplants

❸ *Eleotris sandwicensis*
ʻOʻopu ʻAkupa

Description
The ʻoʻopu ʻakupa is usually a dark brown to black in color. It is one of the larger species of native ʻoʻopu and can reach up to a foot in length. The easiest way to tell this ʻoʻopu apart from the ʻoʻopu nākea, which it superficially resembles is by examining the pelvic fins under its belly. In the ʻoʻopu ʻakupa, the pelvic fins are separate, rather than fused into a disc, as it is in the ʻoʻopu nākea.

Distribution
This ʻoʻopu is endemic to the Hawaiian Islands. It is usually found in the lower reaches of streams, in fresh or brackish water.

Lifestyle
Diet: This ʻoʻopu is an ambush predator. It will hide under rocks and in the mud and leaf litter, darting out to capture fishes that swim by. One of the authors (M. Yamamoto) observed a foot-long ʻoʻopu ʻakupa in a Molokaʻi estuary choking on an ʻoʻopu nākea *(Awaous stamineus)* that was almost as large as it was. This ʻoʻopu is also an opportunistic feeder, often stuffing itself with slow-moving snails and clams.

Juvenile ʻoʻopu ʻakupa.

Breeding: This ʻoʻopu has a breeding cycle that is very similar to that of all our other native freshwater ʻoʻopu. A pair will deposit their eggs on the side or underside of a rock. The eggs are very tiny, measuring no more than a millimeter in length, but a single spawn will number in the thousands. The male will guard the eggs for the short period of time (24-30 hours) that the eggs need to develop and hatch.

Interesting Facts

Traditionally, this ʻoʻopu was caught with a baited hook attached to a short stick, which the fisherman would dip into the water as he moved from rock to rock in the streambed—a fishing method referred to as kiomoʻomo. The ʻakupa was relished lāwalu style over hot coals. Today, this ʻoʻopu is prized as bait by nearshore pāpio fishermen.

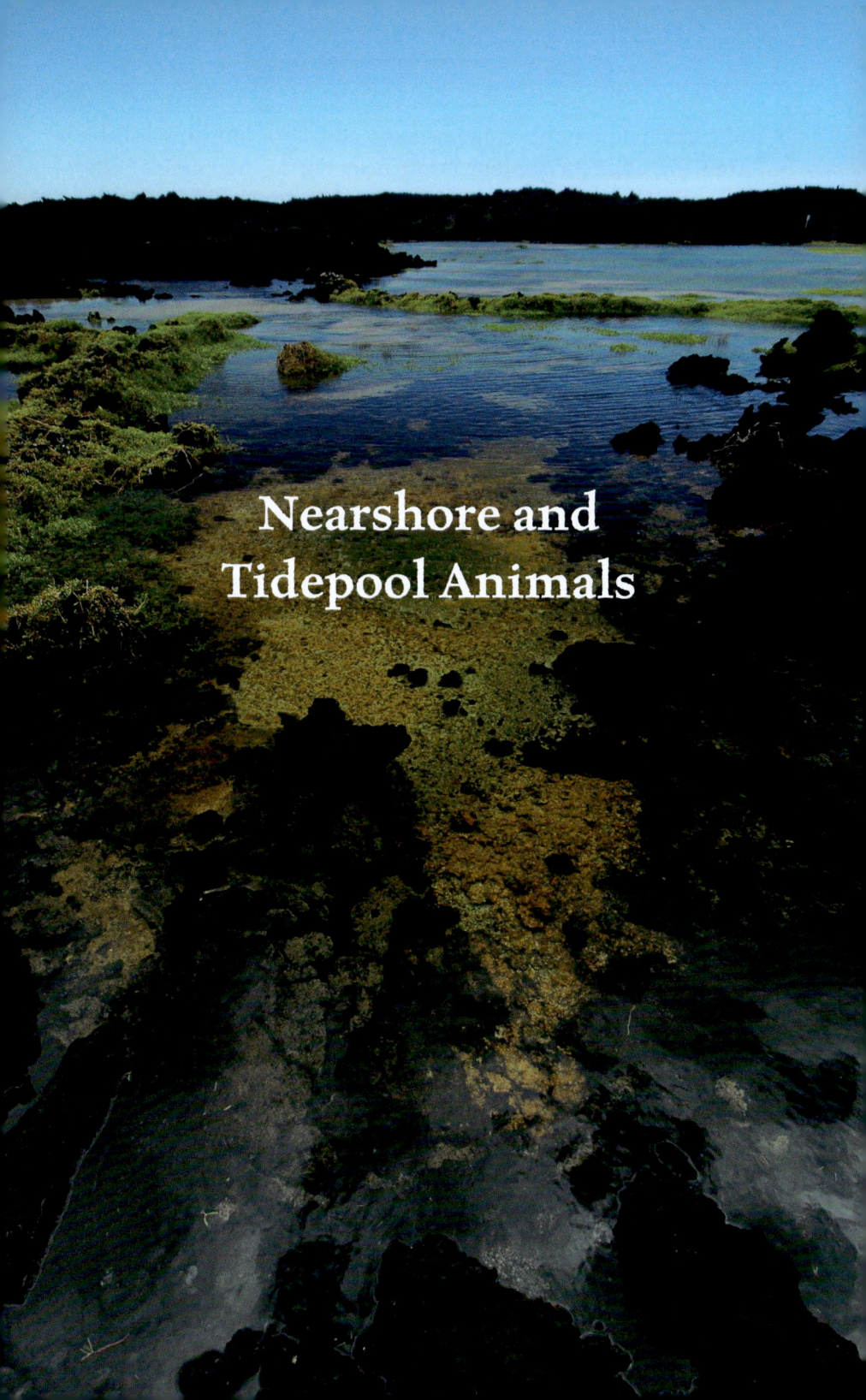

Nearshore and Tidepool Animals

Some anchialine pools contain fauna and flora indistinguishable from the adjacent shoreline and neighboring tidepools. Fishes such as the āholehole, kūpīpī, mamo, and manini are often found in such pools. Their presence suggests that these fishes, along with various shoreline invertebrates and algae, manage to find their way into anchialine pools through one of several ways: 1) through subterranean openings leading to pools that are large enough to allow entry; 2) via high surf where they are transported by wave and surf action; or 3) high tide conditions where the incoming tides carry them into the pools. More information on these incidental anchialine pool residents can be found in many excellent books on Hawaiian nearshore and tidepool animals.

There is also a species of moray eel that is sometimes found in anchialine pools. Historically known as *Gymnothorax hilonis*, this species is more correctly referred to as *G. pictus* or puhi kāpʻā. This eel's habit of hunting above the waterline on reef flats and along

Peppered Moray, Puhi kāpʻā, *Gymnothorax pictus,* **dark color form.** *Photo by John E. Randall.*

Nearshore and Tidepool Animals

Mamo, *Abudefduf abdominalis*. Photo by Kevin Imai.

the shoreline is probably the reason it sometimes finds its way into anchialine pools. What is unique about this eel species is that it is one of the few moray eels that are known to tolerate brackish water environments. Although mostly found on the Big Island, one specimen was collected at Sandy Beach on Oʻahu by a good friend of ours, the late Darrell Takaoka. The puhi kāpʻa is whitish to brown in color with a pattern of finely speckled black dots covering the entire body. However, in brackish water environments like anchialine pools, they take on a darker coloration blending more easily with the basaltic substrate of Big Island anchialine pools.

There's an interesting connection between shoreline fishes such as the āholehole and ʻūʻū or menpachi and our anchialine pool shrimp. One of the favorite prey items of these fishes is shrimp. Since both āholehole and menpachi are typically found in caves and crevices along the shoreline, it's easy to see how they might feed on any anchialine pool shrimp that might get flushed into the ocean on a receding tide.

We received a report from a fisherman who found ʻōpae ʻula in the stomach of an āholehole he caught along the shoreline off Allen Davis Beach (East Oʻahu). This information was significant, because this is

Biology of Anchialine Pools

School of Āholehole, *Kuhlia xenura*. Photo by John E. Randall.

one part of Oʻahu where there have been several reported sightings of ʻōpae ʻula, but with only one confirmed and documented collection of a specimen in the late 1990s. No other specimens have been seen or collected since then. Specimens from this area would provide a missing piece of the puzzle regarding the population genetics of ʻōpae ʻula on Oʻahu. Unfortunately, we were not able to obtain the specimens from the fisherman who caught the āholehole to confirm the identity of the shrimp. It did, however, give us renewed hope that populations of ʻōpae ʻula might someday be found in East Oʻahu, and suggested another way to look for these animals—by examining the gut contents of shoreline fishes such as the āholehole and menpachi.

It was previously believed that there was only one species of āholehole in Hawaiʻi, *Kuhlia sandvicensis*. In addition to collecting the first specimen of *G. pictus* on Oʻahu, Darrell Takaoka was also one of the first to recognize that there was a second species of āholehole. Today, that species is known as *Kuhlia xenura*. One distinguishing characteristic is its eye, which is larger than that of *K. sandvicensis*. *Kuhlia xenura* is also the species of āholehole often found in the lower reaches of freshwater streams. Among his friends, we just know it as Darrell's āholehole.

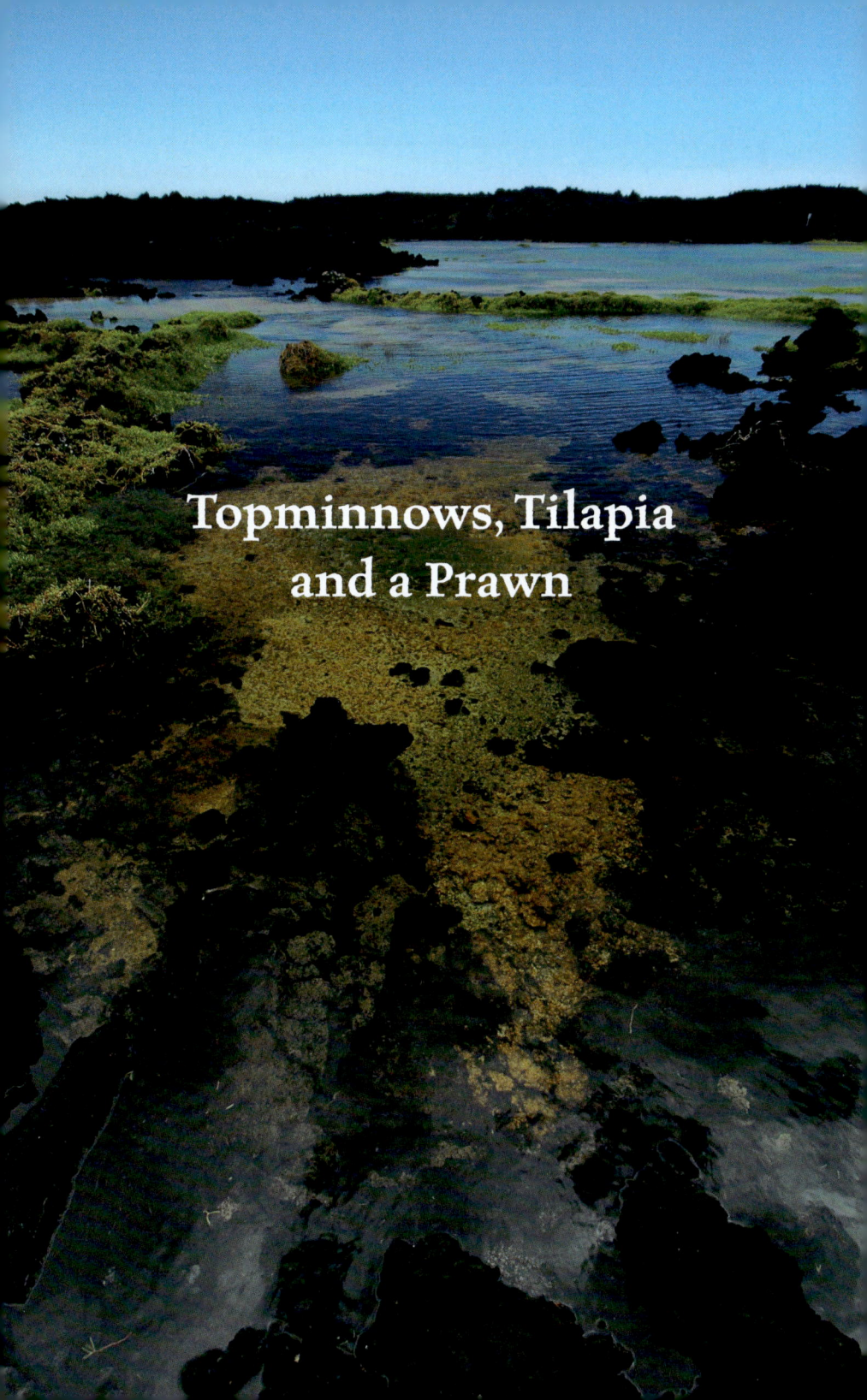

Topminnows, Tilapia and a Prawn

Biology of Anchialine Pools

The exotic animals most often found in anchialine pools include species from two groups of fishes: 1) topminnows originating from Mexico and Central America; 2) various species of tilapia from Africa, and the Tahitian prawn from French Polynesia. All of these animals can tolerate brackish water.

Topminnow a.k.a. Liberty mollies, *Poecilia* sp.

As a group, topminnows include some of the most abundant exotic species found in our streams, reservoirs and estuaries. They are members of the Family Poeciliidae, and include fishes such as the guppy, moonfish, swordtail and molly. One of the reasons that this group is so successful is that they are livebearers. Once the female is inseminated, the fertilized eggs are held within her body for the one month long gestation period. When the young are born, they are large enough to feed and fend for themselves.

Tilapias are another group of exotic fishes that have been very successful in colonizing our fresh, brackish and nearshore waters. They belong to the Family Cichlidae, which includes a wide range of species, such as the angelfish, popular in the aquarium trade, and the tucunare—a highly sought-after gamefish. Although cichlids produce eggs, which are susceptible to predation, most cichlids

Black Chin Tilapia, *Sarotherodon melanotheron.*

deposit their eggs in nests, which one or both parents guard. Many cichlids, including some species of tilapia, take this one step further by incubating their eggs in their mouths. The newly-hatched fry are protected until they can swim and feed on their own.

Since topminnows and tilapia cannot naturally colonize anchialine pools, their presence in anchialine pools means that they were intentionally placed there. One reason topminnows are sometimes released in anchialine pools is for mosquito control. While this point has been debated, it is true that the larvae of some species of mosquitos can tolerate brackish water. One man-made anchialine pool the authors observed in ʻEwa was teeming with mosquito larvae. Although tilapias also feed on mosquito larvae, they are more often released in anchialine pools for fishing purposes or vegetation control. Both topminnows and tilapias are sometimes stocked to provide a source of bait for shoreline fishermen. Unfortunately, these exotic fishes feed on ʻōpae ʻula and other anchialine pool shrimp. When they are introduced, the shrimp disappear.

As its common name implies, the Tahitian prawn is not native to Hawaiʻi. It naturally occurs in French Polynesia, and was introduced as a food resource to Hawai'i from Guam in 1956. Ninety-four specimens were released into Pelekunu Stream on Moloka'i, and a year later, twenty-seven specimens were released into Nu'uanu Stream on O'ahu. Numerous stream surveys were subsequently conducted to determine if the introduction was successful, but for almost ten years not a single specimen was sighted. In 1969 a large specimen was caught in a Big Island stream. Many additional sightings quickly followed. Unlike exotic topminnows and tilapia, the Tahitian prawn's amphidromous lifestyle allowed it to colonize streams and anchialine pools statewide all on its own. These prawns are also incredible climbers, an ability which allows this prawn to colonize the upper reaches of streams.

The Tahitian prawn can grow to more than 6 inches in length. The shell can be bluish-black, reddish brown or even yellowish in color. The pincers are long, thin, bluish-black and curved at the ends. Tahitian prawns are omnivorous, and will no doubt feed on anchialine pool shrimp if given a chance.

Although the terms 'shrimp' and 'prawn' are often used interchangeably, there are differences between these two closely related groups of crustaceans. Prawns are usually larger than shrimp, and have proportionally longer legs. In prawns, the second pair of walking legs has developed into a pair of larger pincers, whereas in shrimp the first pair of legs has the largest pincers. Prawns also have lamellar or plate-like gills, while shrimp have branching gills.

Tahitian Prawn, *Macrobrachium lar*.

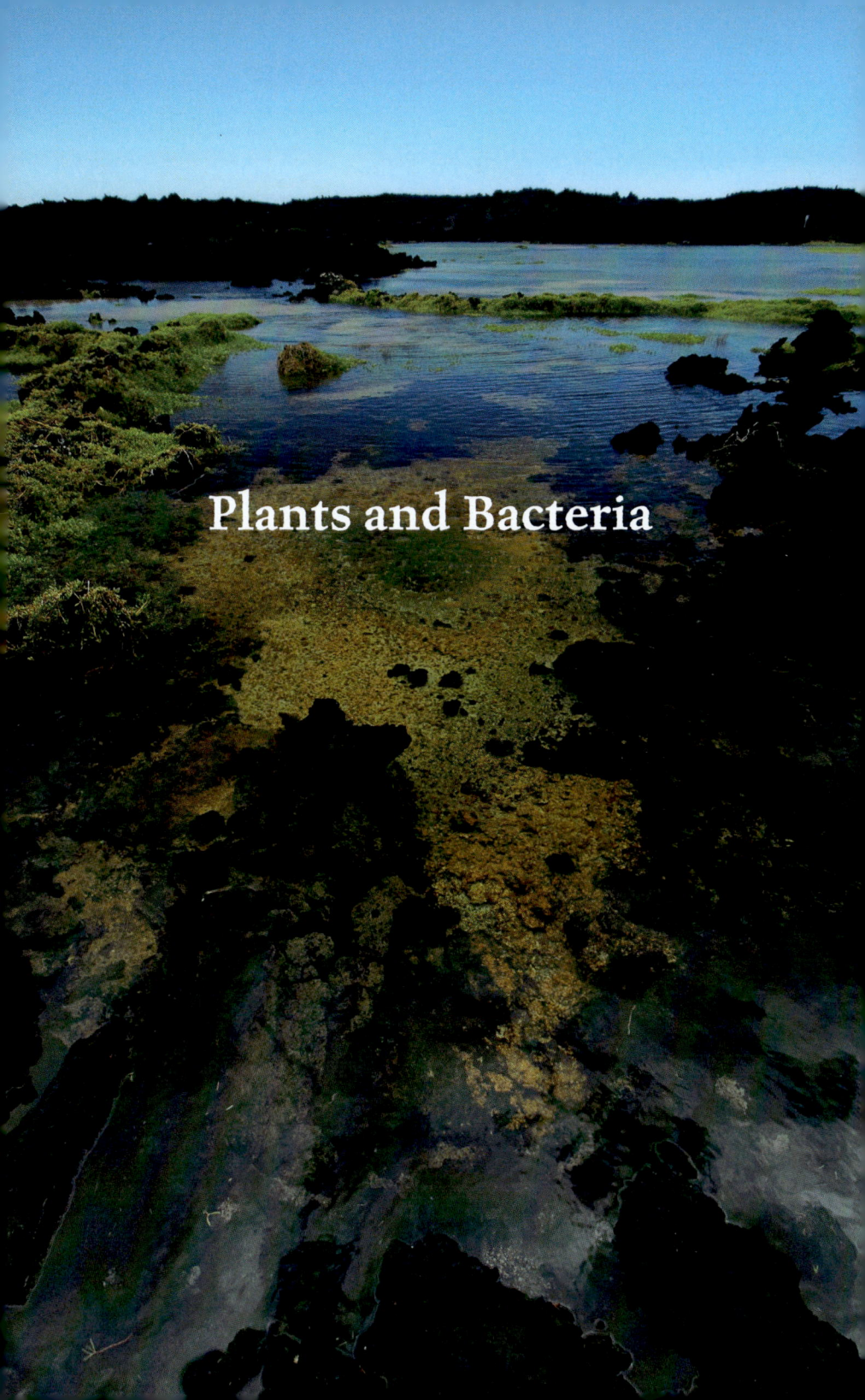

Plants and Bacteria

There are two groups of plants that play important roles in anchialine pools. The first is a flowering plant called *Ruppia maritima*. Commonly called widgeon grass, this plant occurs worldwide in both freshwater and saltwater. It has long, thin, thread-like leaves that can grow several feet long. In anchialine pools, it provides shelter and grazing surfaces for insects, mollusks, 'ōpae 'ula and other small crustaceans.

Anchialine pool with widgeon grass, *Ruppia maritima* and 'ōpae 'ula. *Photo by Alan Cressler.*

Closer view of widgeon grass, *Ruppia maritima,* in a shallow anchialine pool.

At the other end of the evolutionary scale are a number of different species of algae and bacteria which collectively form the orange crust found in many Kona and Maui anchialine pools. Referred to as a cyanobacterial crust, this algal-bacterial complex provides shelter and food for ʻōpae ʻula and other anchialine pool animals.

Anchialine pool in Kaʻū, Hawaiʻi with orange cyanobacterial crust. *Photo by Alan Cressler.*

Photo illustrating the thin and fragile nature of the orange cyanobacterial crust in an anchialine pool at ʻĀhihi-Kīnaʻu, Maui, Hawaiʻi.

Biogeography of Anchialine Pool Shrimp

Calliasmata pholidota.

In 1968, an earthquake opened up a great crack in the earth. The crack, measuring over a hundred feet long and almost five feet wide, revealed a large body of water. When divers entered the water, they discovered that the water was brackish, even though it was more than 400 feet from the ocean. They found a myriad of aquatic life normally found in the ocean, such as algae, sponges, worms, mussels and shrimp. One of these was a blind, cave dwelling shrimp later identified as *Calliasmata pholidota*—the same species found in anchialine pools on Maui and the Big Island. What made this discovery remarkable, was that this crack was located close to a town called Ras Mohammed, on the Sinai Peninsula in Egypt.

How could it be that *Calliasmata pholidota* can occur in two locations, halfway around the world from each other? Another anchialine pool shrimp, *Antecaridina lauensis,* has been found in the Solomon and Ryukyu Islands, and more recently, *Metabetaeus lohena,* was discovered on Easter Island, approximately 4,500 miles south-east of Hawai'i. This extremely disjunct distribution pattern has puzzled scientists for a long time. Dr. John Maciolek, formerly of the Hawai'i Cooperative Fishery Research Unit at the University of Hawai'i, was a pioneer in the study of Hawaiian anchialine pools. He hypothesized that since these anchialine pool shrimp live out of sight in the subterranean, or hypogeal environment, they may occur in many other intermediate locations, yet undiscovered. This could provide 'stepping stones' between the presently known, widely separated locations, making colonization via ocean dispersed larvae much more plausible.

Two *Antecaridina lauensis* and one *Halocaridina rubra*.

Closer to home, there are equally puzzling mysteries related to the distribution of these anchialine pool shrimp. We know for example, that 'ōpae 'ula on the different islands, and even on different parts of the same island, can differ slightly in size and appearance. Since anchialine pools can have very different physical properties, we often wondered if the 'ōpae 'ula living in them were genetically different. In Lua O Palahemo, for example, the 'ōpae 'ula found there were once believed to be a different species and named *Halocaridina palahemo*.

Twenty years ago these questions would have remained largely unanswered. Today, as viewers of modern crime dramas can tell you, the science of DNA has changed everything. If unraveling the mysteries of 'ōpae 'ula genetics is somewhat akin to solving a murder mystery, then the 'Ōpae 'Ula CSI Unit is located in, of all places, The Santos Lab, on the campus of Auburn University, in Auburn, Alabama.

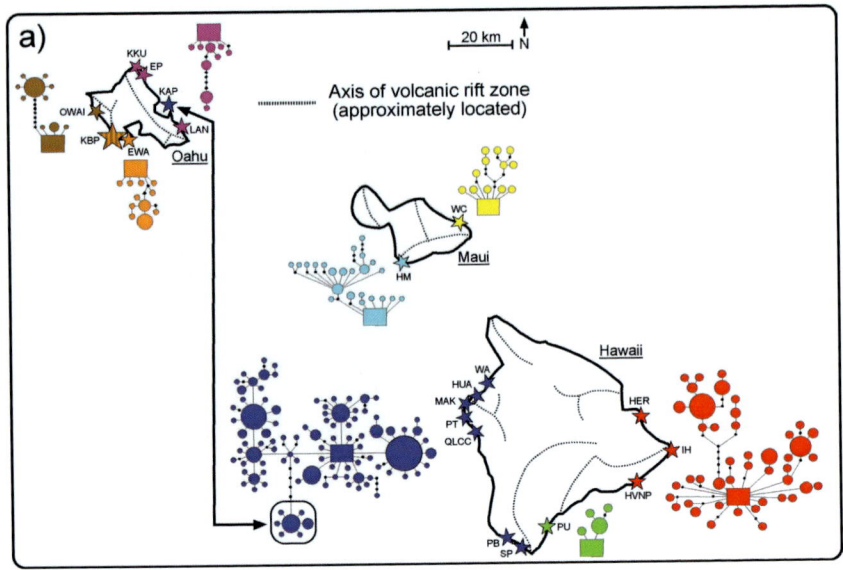

Lineages of 'ōpae 'ula statewide. Copyright 2014 by the Association for the Sciences of Limnology and Oceanography, Inc., Craft et al., 2008.

Dr. Scott Santos is a Maui boy who is an Associate Professor of Biological Sciences at Auburn University. He has specialized in DNA analysis, and particularly as it applies to the field of population genetics. Fortunately for us, and because of his Island roots, Scott is very familiar with anchialine pools, and well aware of how DNA analysis may be able to answer many of the questions we have about 'ōpae 'ula population dynamics.

Dr. Santos and his staff have collected and analyzed the DNA of 'ōpae 'ula from 20 different locations throughout the State. This data is presented in the Diagram above. They discovered that at least 8 genetically distinct populations or 'lineages' of 'ōpae 'ula exists statewide (represented by the different colors). Three of these lineages are on the Big Island: West Hawai'i, Ka'ū and East Hawai'i; two are on Maui: East Maui and South Maui, and three are on O'ahu: West O'ahu, Windward O'ahu and South O'ahu. Remarkably, one population of 'ōpae 'ula found on Kapapa Island (KAP) in Kāne'ohe Bay on O'ahu is genetically identical to the West Hawai'i lineage. Since O'ahu is much older than the Big Island, it is likely that the West Hawai'i lineage was established by 'ōpae 'ula larvae that somehow made its way from Kapapa Island in Kāne'ohe Bay to the Kona Coast, rather than the

Dr. Scott Santos and authors Thomas Iwai Jr. and Annette Tagawa collecting ōpae'ula for DNA analysis.

other way around. This also suggests that the Big Island was colonized at least twice, since another group of larvae must have established the East Hawai'i lineage. Another surprise was that the anchialine pool complex at Kalaeloa (KBP) on O'ahu contains a mixture of West O'ahu and South O'ahu 'ōpae 'ula. This is the only pool complex statewide, known to contain 'ōpae 'ula from two different lineages.

There are several other fascinating 'takeaways' from Scott's data. Each colored circle represents a unique DNA sequence recovered within a particular lineage (color). The larger the circle, the higher the frequency of that particular DNA sequence found in the samples. Each rectangle represents the DNA sequence believed to be the most ancestral in that particular lineage. The lines connecting any two circles represents a single mutational difference in the DNA sequences. The small, black circles are 'placeholders' for DNA sequences that have not been sampled, but thought to exist, either today or in the past. They represent the intermediate steps linking the two sampled DNA sequences. Finally, Dr. Santos' data indicate that the mitochondrial DNA differences between the different 'ōpae 'ula lineages is about 5%.

Dr. Robert Kinzie III and Atlantis Russ preparing to collect samples of *Metabetaeus lohena*.
Photo by Scott R. Santos.

To put this into context, the mitochondrial DNA differences between humans and chimpanzees is about 9%. Is a 5% difference enough to distinguish each of these 8 lineages as 8 different species?

Atlantis Russ, another colleague from the University of Hawai'i at Hilo, conducted a similar analysis of *Metabetaeus lohena* populations throughout the State. After examining the DNA from 127 specimens from 7 locations on the Islands of O'ahu, Maui and the Big Island, Atlantis discovered that the situation with *Metabetaeus* is exactly the opposite—only one lineage of *M. lohena* exists statewide.

These results are amazing, but they raise the question of why there are so many different lineages of 'ōpae 'ula, but only one lineage of *Metabetaeus lohena*. Part of the answer lies with the different reproductive strategies of these two species.

'Ōpae 'ula produce relatively few, large eggs. The resulting larvae are large in size and possess a big yolk sac. These lecithotrophic larvae are sustained throughout their larval development by their yolk reserves—they do not have to feed. Lecithotrophic larvae typically spend a short period of time (about 4 weeks) drifting about as they

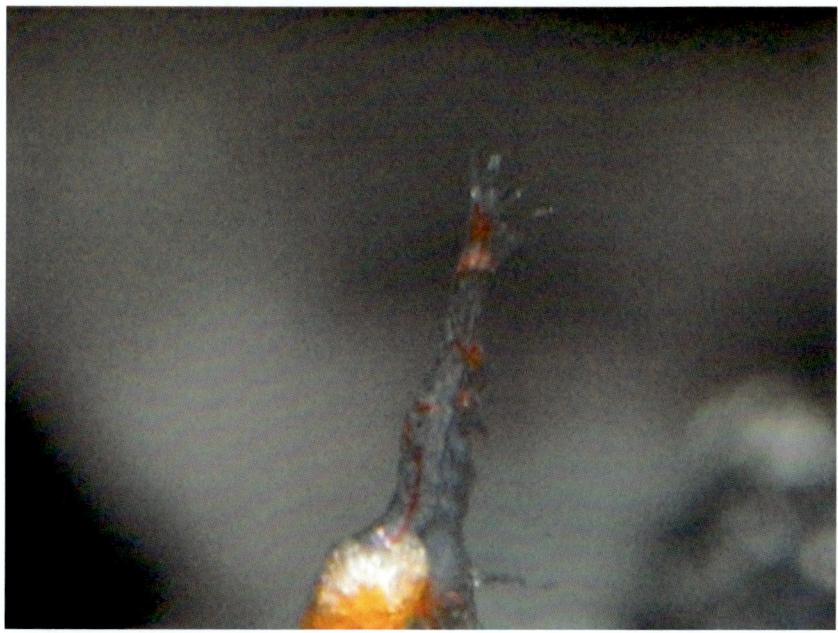

'Ōpae 'ula, larva with yolk sac.

develop, before settling out as post-larvae. Clearly, if 'ōpae 'ula can complete their life cycle in a tiny micro-habitat, generations of these animals can probably do the same within the relative confines of their anchialine pool complex. The inability of 'ōpae 'ula larvae to travel long distances restricts the exchange and mixing of DNA between different populations of 'ōpae 'ula. As we have seen with many different plant and animal groups here in Hawai'i, genetic isolation is one of the prime driving forces for the evolution of new species.

Metabetaeus lohena, by contrast, produce more eggs that are smaller in size. The resulting planktotrophic larvae possess small yolk reserves. Once absorbed, these larvae must feed to continue their development. Their need to find food suggests that *Metabetaeus* larvae leave the anchialine pool complex and become part of the oceanic plankton as they develop. Planktotrophic larvae typically have a longer larval development phase, and consequently have the potential to travel longer distances before they settle out. This is probably the reason *Metabetaeus lohena* populations statewide are genetically similar—there is a regular exchange and mixture of DNA

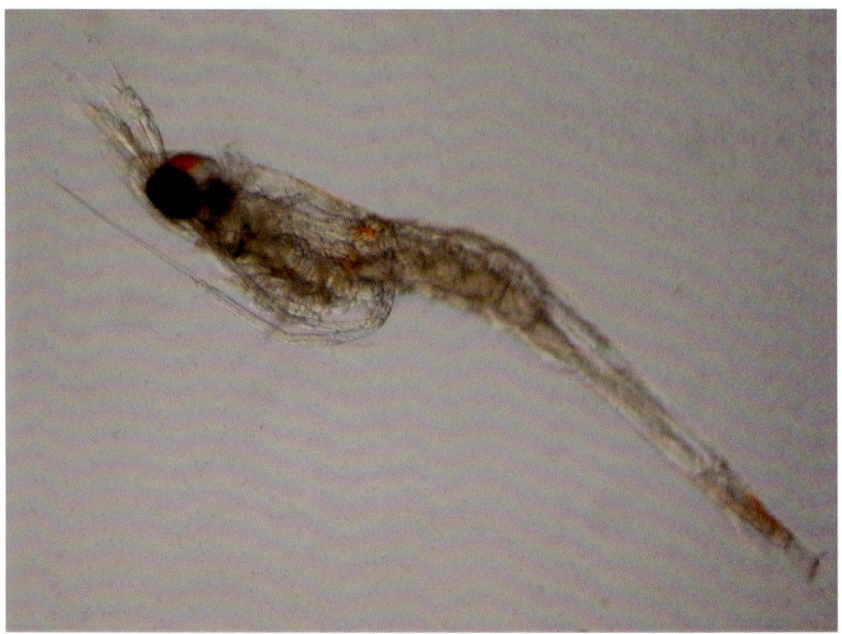

Metabetaeus lohena larva.

between the different populations. This difference in reproductive strategies between the ʻōpae ʻula and *Metabetaeus lohena* could also explain why ʻōpae ʻula are much more abundant than *M. lohena*. Although ʻōpae ʻula produce fewer eggs, their larvae are much more likely to survive than the far ranging *M. lohena* larvae, which must beat difficult odds to make it back to an anchialine pool.

There may also be physical barriers isolating populations of ʻōpae ʻula. In the Diagram on page 70 showing the lineages of the ʻōpae ʻula, Dr. Santos has also marked the rift zones on each of the islands. Rift zones are areas where the different volcanoes that make up the island are rifting or splitting apart. These are weak areas where it is easiest for the magma to work its way up to the surface. Solidified columns of magma along these rift zones can form dikes, which have low water permeability, and can serve to restrict ground water flow which in turn restricts the movement of ʻōpae ʻula. As you can see, there is a good correlation between the location of the rift zones, and the boundaries between the different lineages of ʻōpae ʻula.

Threats to Anchialine Pools

Aging anchialine pool filling in with sand and sedimentation.

On a geological time scale, anchialine pools are ephemeral. They are formed in young lava flows or ancient limestone reefs, and gradually fill in with silt and debris over time. Unfortunately, this natural aging process can be greatly accelerated by the activities of man.

Anchialine pools are the lighted or epigeal portions of an anchialine pool ecosystem. These pools provide an important source of food for our subterranean anchialine pool creatures. However, anchialine pools have been impacted by man almost as soon as the first Polynesians settled in these islands more than 1,000 years ago. Pools containing waters with the lower salinities were used for drinking and bathing while larger, higher salinity pools were modified to culture fish. These impacts have greatly increased in modern times. Today, three of the primary threats to anchialine pools include: 1) loss or degradation of habitat; 2) introduction and spread of exotic species; and 3) overharvesting of 'ōpae 'ula for the ornamental pet trade.

Loss or Degradation of Habitat

Urbanization along the Kona Coast on the Big Island and on the 'Ewa Plain on O'ahu have resulted in a major loss of anchialine pool habitats. On the Kona Coast, resort and golf course development have caused the destruction of many of its anchialine pools. On O'ahu, the second city of Kapolei is being built on the 'Ewa Plain—the largest karst formation on the island. Intact and thriving anchialine pools in this area have been destroyed as well. The irreversible loss of habitat caused by the excavation of acres and acres of land along the shoreline for harbor and marina development is clearly devastating for anchialine pool ecosystems.

Construction within the 'Ewa karst, 'Ewa Marina, O'ahu.

In 1975, during construction of the Barbers Point Harbor, one of the most impressive sinkholes ever found on O'ahu was discovered. The large, water-filled cavern was revealed when a bulldozer partially broke through its limestone covering. The cavern's ceiling was covered with stalactites—'icicles' of calcium carbonate formed by dissolved minerals in the groundwater dripping into the cavern. The pool itself was more than 30 feet deep and contained 'ōpae 'ula.

Threats to Anchialine Pools

Entrance to the subterranean anchialine pool discovered during construction at the Barbers Point Harbor, 1977. *Photo by Aki Sinoto, Bishop Museum.*

Dr. Richard Brock happened to be at the Harbor doing some fieldwork on the day this pool was discovered. One can only imagine his excitement at being one of the first persons to view this remarkable sight. The following is Richard's personal account of his encounter with this amazing anchialine pool:

> In October 1975, I, along with four others, were involved with marine environmental field studies carried out in support of the proposed expansion of the (then) Barbers Point Barge Harbor. These studies included work on water chemistry, circulation, phytoplankton, zooplankton, fish and benthic communities to assess the probable impacts that may occur to these communities as well as expected physical changes that would happen with the Harbor's expansion. The Harbor is situated in an elevated fossilized limestone reef (karst) which is porous and could potentially have anchialine pools present. Concurrent with the environmental studies was an effort to do a preliminary clearing and removal of vegetation (kiawe primarily) present on the mauka lands slated to become part of the Harbor.
>
> One morning, I spoke to a bulldozer operator involved with the land clearing and asked if he had seen any holes or other places with standing water (which could indicate the presence of an anchialine pool). The short answer was no but if he came across something, he would let us know. At lunch time, the bulldozer operator came

over and said that he had uncovered "a cave with water in it". On inspection, the bulldozer operator had cut through one side of a limestone dome or "bubble" about 10 m in diameter that had formed a solid "roof" over an anchialine pool that was about 2.5 m below the land surface. The limestone "roof" had completely covered the pool, thus blocking all light. As memory serves, an irregularly-shaped anchialine pool was present, occupying about two-thirds of the cave's floor. This pool was about 7 m in greatest dimension with extremely clear water and initially looked to be about 7 m in apparent depth (actual depth was closer to 10 m). Also present were 'ōpae 'ula *(Halocaridina rubra)* occurring at very low density. Several specimens were collected for the purpose of positive identification and the salinity of the water in the cave was measured at 2.6 ppt.

The location of the pool was shared with Dr. John Maciolek with whom I collaborated and in turn Dr. Maciolek contacted Dr. Alan Ziegler, a vertebrate zoologist at the Bishop Museum. At the bottom of the pool was found a rich deposit of intact bones of extinct birds new to science. Today the cave no longer exists because it was located in the inner reaches of the expanded Barbers Point Harbor basin.

This cavern, known only by its Bishop Museum archaeological site number 'B6-139', is most notably remembered for containing the fossilized remains of a number of extinct Hawaiian birds.

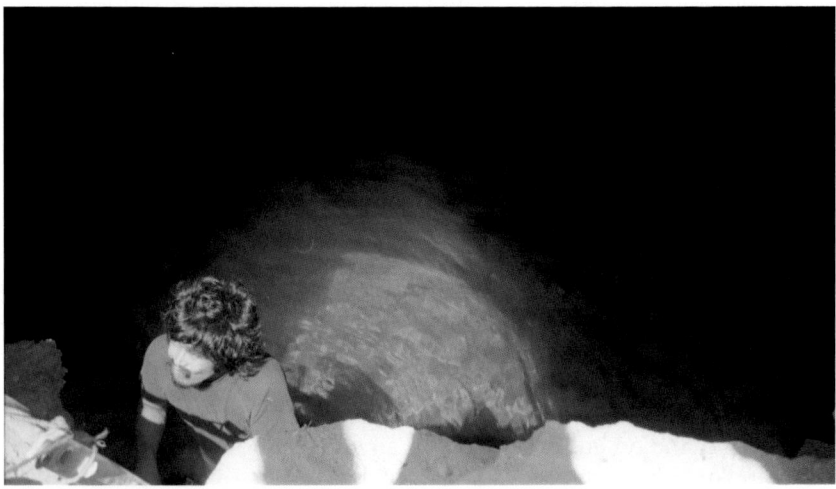

Researcher preparing to survey the B6-139 anchialine pool, 1977.
Photo by Aki Sinoto, Bishop Museum.

Threats to Anchialine Pools

Cave interior with stalactites and partial view of the anchialine pool, 1977.
Photo by Aki Sinoto, Bishop Museum.

Stalactites recovered from the B6-139 sinkhole by Dr. Richard Brock prior to its destruction.
Photo by Richard E. Brock.

Bishop Museum archaeologist, Dr. Aki Sinoto, reported that bulldozer operators had tried to backfill this cave before 1977, but were unsuccessful because it was too large. After an abbreviated archaeological survey was completed by Bishop Museum staff, the pool was destroyed to complete the Harbor. One can only wonder about other anchialine pools, passing into oblivion without even having their presence noted.

One final insult that anchialine pools have suffered is their use as receptacles for trash and human waste. There is only one anchialine pool that we are aware of on the Wai'anae Coast. This pool is important because it is the primary habitat of 'ōpae 'ula from the West O'ahu lineage, and also contains *Metabetaeus lohena*. Since this pool is completely 'dry' on a low tide, to some individuals, it apparently appears to be just a hole in the ground. As a result, this anchialine pool has been repeatedly trashed over the years. While the damage thus far has not been significant, it may be only a matter of time before trash containing toxic substances such as used motor oil, or household cleansers are dumped into the pool. The resulting damage to the pool and underlying water table could be much more serious—perhaps irreversible.

Before: Wai'anae anchialine pool full of trash.

After: Author Thomas Iwai Jr. finds 'ōpae 'ula thriving once again after trash removal several weeks later.

In the 'Āhihi-Kīna'u Natural Area Reseve on Maui, habitat degradation caused by increasing numbers of visitors is a major concern. The reserve was established to keep the area in a pristine and natural condition. It was never intended to support the hundreds of people visiting the reserve daily. Visitors have been leaving behind trash and in some cases, human waste. The presence of people has also disturbed some water birds and sea life causing them to leave. In response, Reserve managers have been forced to restrict access to a large section of the NAR, including the anchialine pools, until a long-term solution to this problem can be found.

Introduction and Spread of Exotic Species

One of the biggest threats that account for the degradation of anchialine pool habitats is the introduction and spread of exotic fishes such as topminnows and tilapia and exotic plants such as the seashore paspalum, *Paspalum vaginatum*. Most notably on the Big Island, exotic fishes have been released into anchialine pools for mosquito control or for ornamental purposes.

When exotic fishes like topminnows and tilapia are introduced into anchialine pools, they will prey upon the 'ōpae 'ula and other anchialine pool shrimp causing them to seek shelter and hide in the dark recesses of the pool, often forcing them back underground into the hypogeal environment. 'Ōpae 'ula will primarily feed on algae which is abundant in the lighted portions of the anchialine pool. However, the presence of predators like topminnows and tilapia can prevent the 'ōpae 'ula from emerging into the lighted portions of the anchialine pool to graze upon the algae. In addition, since these exotic fish have no natural enemies in anchialine pools, they can reproduce in abundance and spread unchecked. This increases the biological load in the pool resulting in uncontrolled algae growth, sedimentation, and the eventual destruction of the anchialine pool.

On Maui, the 'ōpae 'ula in Wai'ānapanapa Cave are threatened by wild guppies, which were probably released into the pool for mosquito control. The 'ōpae 'ula in this cave are culturally significant because they are tied to the legend of a Hawaiian Princess named Popoalaea, who was murdered in the cave by her husband, Chief Kakae. On the

Threats to Anchialine Pools

Wild guppies in the Wai'ānapanapa Cave anchialine pool.

anniversary of her death in the spring, the waters of the cave would reportedly turn blood red in her memory. This phenomenon was supposedly caused by large numbers of 'ōpae 'ula swimming in the water column. Unfortunately, this no longer occurs. The presence of guppies in the open, sun-lit part of the cave have forced the 'ōpae 'ula to retreat to the dark recesses of the cave.

In addition to erosion control and ornamental purposes, seashore paspalum is a popular grass used for golf course turf in Hawai'i because of its resistance to salt spray. It will grow nicely with the use of lower salinity water for irrigation. This is especially desirable in areas where freshwater is a precious commodity since it provides a low cost alternative for irrigation. In addition, most weeds cannot tolerate lower salinity water which helps to keep maintenance costs to a minimum. However, in areas where seashore paspalum is planted near anchialine pools, it can become a problem by taking over the natural vegetation surrounding these pools and has even been found growing completely submerged within the pools. Once this grass is established in an anchialine pool, it is virtually impossible to remove. Hence, it is strongly recommended that all future developments being planned around or near anchialine pools consider using an

Golf course putting green with seashore paspalum.

alternative grass instead of seashore paspalum for areas where grass is to be included as part of the landscape design.

Overharvesting for the Pet Trade

ʻŌpae ʻula are currently being harvested in large numbers for the pet trade. They are commonly sold as pets in 'biospheres' and other micro-habitats, and also as live food for seahorses and other marine and freshwater fishes. While we personally feel that there is some redeeming value for their use as pets, it is extremely wasteful to use these very unique animals for fish food.

Healthy and intact anchialine pools could easily sustain a reasonable level of harvest of ʻōpae ʻula. Unfortunately, most of our anchialine pools are not healthy. On the Kona Coast, where all of the reported harvesting occurs, approximately 90% of the anchialine pools have been impacted by alien species. It is therefore of critical importance for resource managers to determine the level of harvest that is sustainable, and to develop the regulations and inspection protocols needed to insure that these levels are not exceeded.

Threats to Anchialine Pools

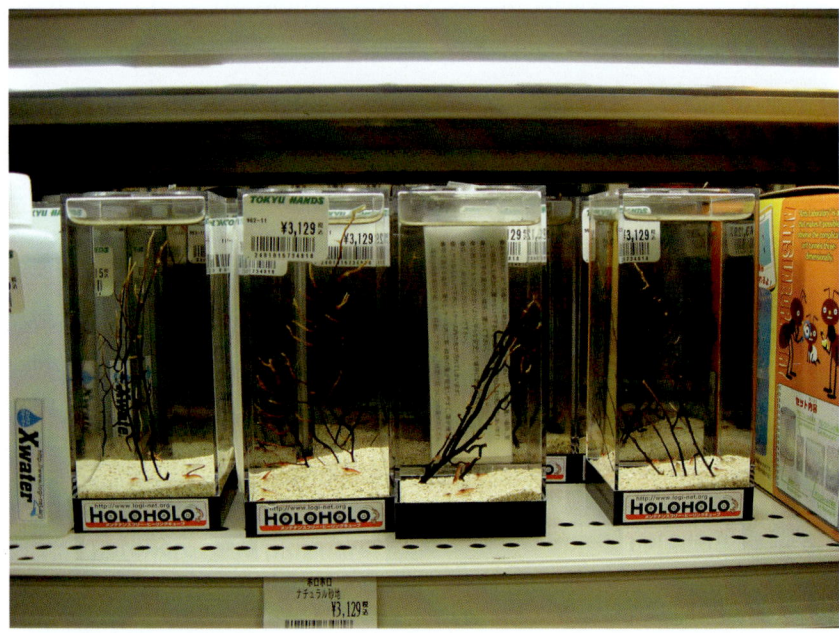

'Ōpae 'ula micro-habitats for sale in Japan.

'Ōpae 'ula micro-habitats for sale in a local department store.

Habitat Restoration

Big Island

Habitat restoration efforts on the Big Island have followed several different paths. In areas where resort development have resulted in the destruction of anchialine pools, restoration efforts have been focused on creating new anchialine pools to replace those destroyed by construction. Since the animals are present in the water table, creation of a new anchialine pool simply consists of digging a hole deep enough to reach the water table. Some of these resorts have discovered that anchialine pools are a valuable asset, and have developed educational programs built around them with trained staff.

The destruction of anchialine pools by developers is no longer carried out as freely and easily as it once was. Today state and federal officials recognize the classification of anchialine pool waters as Class AA waters which means that the water in anchialine pools is considered natural and pristine. Under the Clean Water Act, Class AA waters are to be remained in their natural pristine state as much as possible with an absolute minimum of any activities that could

Anchialine Pool Preservation Area on the grounds of the Waikoloa Beach Marriot Resort & Spa on the Big Island.

Habitat Restoration

Restored anchialine pool at the Four Seasons Resort at Hualālai, Kailua-Kona, Hawai'i.

With proper management, anchialine pools can coexist alongside development.

Habitat Restoration

Anchialine pool fallen victim to exotic fish introductions resulting in the overgrowth of plants, algae and sedimentation.

possibly pollute and/or alter the water quality of these anchialine pool environments. This classification makes it illegal to fill in or alter any anchialine pool without a permit. In addition, during the environmental review process for any development activities near anchialine pool habitats, mitigative measures for protecting and preventing contaminants such as sediments, pollutants, petroleum products and other debris from possibly entering the aquatic environment must be addressed before pemits are issued.

Efforts have also been made to restore anchialine pools that have been degraded by the introduction of exotic plants and fishes. These ponds are often filled with large masses of plants, covered by a thick layer of sediment, and populated by exotic fishes that prey upon the anchialine pool shrimp. In these situations, restoration efforts consist of removing the exotic plants and fishes, and pumping out the accumulated sediment. One of the biggest problems has been the lack of an effective piscicide (fish poison) that is approved for use in anchialine pools. Rotenone has been used effectively in the past, but there are legal constraints to its use today.

Maui

Thanks to the foresight of State officials in establishing the first Natural Area Reserve at ʻĀhihi-Kīnaʻu in 1973, this anchialine pool complex is still relatively pristine.

ʻĀhihi-Kīnaʻu Natural Area Reserve, Maui, Hawaiʻi.

Unfortunately, the same cannot be said for the Waiʻānapanapa Cave anchialine pool, which is contaminated with wild guppies, *Poecilia reticulata*. Waiʻānapanapa Cave is a unique anchialine pool system. The water is cold, and almost completely fresh. ʻŌpae ʻula are still present, but they are restricted to the dark recesses of the cave. The guppies, which were apparently introduced for mosquito control, live in the front, sunlit part of the pool. Attempts by Skippy Hau, DAR's Maui Biologist, to physically remove these guppies with nets have proved unsuccessful. There are just too many nooks and crannies in the cave, and since guppies are livebearers, a single, missed, gravid female would negate the entire effort. One of the authors (M. Yamamoto) proposed a biological control approach that he believed entailed few risks, but unfortunately, was not given the opportunity to try it. The current situation, with the exotic guppies in the front of the cave, and the ʻōpae ʻula confined to the back of the cave, is therefore likely to persist into the foreseeable future.

Habitat Restoration

Aerial view of the Kalaeloa Unit of the Pearl Harbor National Wildlife Refuge, Oʻahu.

Oʻahu

While there are few anchialine pools on Oʻahu, there are many shoreline areas where these animals are known to be present in the groundwater. One such area is the Kalaeloa Unit of the Pearl Harbor National Wildlife Refuge (NWR). The Kalaeloa Unit covers 37 acres of the south-west corner of the former Barbers Point Naval Air Station It was added to the NWR in 2001 to protect the last remaining coastal dry shrubland plant communities on Oʻahu.

In 2003, a small sinkhole was discovered by NWR staff. Unlike the other sinkholes in the NWR, which had been filled with soil and limestone rubble, this one was still open. This sinkhole was 4 to 5 feet deep, and during high tides, there was a small pool of water on the bottom containing ʻōpae ʻula. After discussions with NWR staff, we decided to excavate additional sinkholes in the refuge to determine if the restored sinkholes would be colonized by ʻōpae ʻula, and possibly other species of anchialine pool shrimp.

The NWR is roughly triangular in shape, with the south side of the triangle forming part of the shoreline, and the west side abutting the drainage canal that separates it from Campbell Industrial Park. After surveying the area, we selected a dozen potential sites for excavation, half on the canal side of the refuge, and the other half on the seaward side.

A unique aspect of this restoration project was that it represented a cooperative effort between the U.S. Fish and Wildlife Service, the State of Hawai'i, and private industry. As managers of the NWR, the U.S. Fish and Wildlife Service maintained overall control and management of the project. We served as advisors, and were responsible for monitoring the restored sinkholes, and private industry, represented by a crew from Hawaiian Dredging and Construction (HD&C) would provide the manpower and heavy equipment to do the actual excavation.

Excavation of Sinkhole #3 at Kalaeloa NWR.

The restoration work took place on January 15, 2005. During the 4 to 5 hours that the HD&C crew was available, three sinkholes were excavated. Sinkholes #1 and #2 were located 50 and 100 feet, respectively, from the canal. Both were excavated to a depth of 10 feet, which was the maximum reach of the excavator. Both sinkholes showed no signs of water infiltration. Sinkhole #3 was located on the seaward side of the refuge, approximately 100 feet from the highwater mark, and in close proximity to the natural sinkhole discovered in 2003. At a depth of approximately 7 feet, the excavator reached the water table and groundwater began seeping into the hole.

Habitat Restoration

Water depth at 2 feet in Sinkhole #3.

Successful restoration of Sinkhole #3 with concentrations of ʻōpae ʻula along the edges of the pool.

Habitat Restoration

After the excavation work was complete, the restored sinkholes were surveyed on a monthly basis. Sinkhole #1 remained dry and was backfilled after four months. Sinkhole #2 experienced some infiltration of ground water, but the water was brown with tannins and foul smelling. This sinkhole was also eventually backfilled. Sinkhole #3 by contrast, displayed excellent groundwater infiltration. On high tides, water depth in this sinkhole reached 2 feet. Nine months after restoration, the first 'ōpae 'ula were discovered in Sinkhole #3. These first 'ōpae 'ula were not small, newly recruited juvenile shrimp, but full grown adults. This suggested to us that 'ōpae 'ula were present in the water table close to the newly restored sinkhole. Why did it take 9 months for the 'ōpae 'ula to appear in the sinkhole? Perhaps it took that long for groundwater flow and tidal forces to flush the sediment from the subterranean cracks and crevices.

Based on the success of this initial restoration effort, Lorena 'Tap' Wada, Aaron Nadig and their staff from the USFWS restored 12 additional sinkholes in the NWR between 2006 and 2008. All of the sinkholes were in close proximity to the natural sinkhole and Sinkhole #3, on the seaward side of the NWR. After the excavation process, one additional step was taken to hasten the natural flushing

Excavation of 12 additional sinkholes by USFWS staff.

Habitat Restoration

Matthew Ramsey and Lorena Wada preparing to flush excess silt from an excavated pool. *Photo by Aaron Nadig.*

Jeff Herod, Lorena Wada and Joy Hiromasa Browning in the process of flushing the excavated pool with a water pump. *Photo by Aaron Nadig.*

Authors Thomas Iwai Jr. and Mike Yamamoto assist with the flushing and removal of silt from an excavated pool. *Photo by Aaron Nadig.*

process and remove silt from the restored pools. A top-mount slip-on pick-up truck mounted fire pumper unit was used to blast freshwater into the sides and bottom of the pools to dislodge as much silt as possible. A trash water pump was then used to remove the silt-laden water.

'Ōpae 'ula first began appearing in these 12 restored sinkholes after just 2 to 3 months—a significant reduction from the 9 months it took for 'ōpae 'ula to colonize Sinkhole #3. The use of the fire pumper unit to accelerate the natural flushing process apparently made a big difference. In 2010, the first *Metabetaeus lohena* appeared approximately 10 months after the pool was restored. Today, all 13 of the restored pools have 'ōpae 'ula in them, and 8 of these pools, including Sinkhole #3, have *Metabetaeus lohena.*

Thanks to the efforts of Lorena, Aaron and the USFWS staff, the NWR at Kalaeloa now has the biggest concentration of anchialine pools on O'ahu.

Habitat Restoration

Close up view of 'ōpae 'ula recruitment at Kalaeloa restored sinkhole.

New generations of stewards can now learn about anchialine pool ecology at Kalaeloa.

Biospheres and Micro-Habitats

In an age of pet rocks, virtual pets, robotic dogs and other low maintenance pets, it's easy to understand the popularity of 'biospheres' and other micro-habitats containing 'ōpae 'ula. If properly set-up, they are fascinating to watch and require very little care.

DAR Secretary Lorraine Takaoka and Fisheries Data Aid Nikky Siu admire Lorraine's 'ōpae 'ula crack seed jar.

The term biosphere refers to that part of the earth and it's atmosphere where all living things exist. Plants take nutrients and water from the soil, carbon dioxide from the air and light energy from the sun to produce the food and oxygen that animals consume. The waste products generated by the animals, and the carbon dioxide that they exhale are then re-used by plants. Micro-habitats mimic a very tiny part of the biosphere by using algae in the role of the primary producers (plants), and 'ōpae 'ula as the consumers (animals).

The popularity of these micro-habitats is a double-edged sword for resource managers. One positive benefit is that they generate an awareness and appreciation of these animals and the habitat in which they live. A live exhibit of 'ōpae 'ula located inside the visitor center of the Hawai'i Volcanoes National Park was designed to highlight

Biospheres and Micro-Habitats

Live exhibit of 'ōpae 'ula located at the visitor center of the Hawai'i Volcanoes National Park.
Photo courtesy of David Fukumoto.

anchialine pool ecosystems within the Park. This exhibit was a collaborative effort between Park Ranger Dean Gallagher and David Fukumoto of the Fuku-Bonsai Cultural Center in an effort to educate visitors about these unique shrimp and the anchialine pools that they inhabit.

Micro-habitats are easy and inexpensive for teachers to setup and maintain, and make excellent tools for students to learn the basic concepts of ecology. Many of the scientists in this field today were inspired to become biologists and ecologists by keeping and observing similar micro-habitats – some of us still do. The problem is that the popularity of these micro-habitats has resulted in the increased collection of 'ōpae 'ula for the pet trade.

Our purpose in writing this chapter was not to encourage or discourage the keeping of these micro-habitats, but to provide suggestions to interested individuals to maximize their chances for success. The micro-habitat in the photo on page 96 was set up by our secretary, Lorraine Takaoka. It produced hundreds of baby 'ōpae 'ula over the years, which she provided to others who set up micro-habitats of their own. If Lorraine's success could be duplicated, it's easy to see how captive bred 'ōpae 'ula could help to reduce the need to harvest wild stocks.

Although 'ōpae 'ula can survive in a very small amount of water, bigger is definitely better. Larger volumes of water are more resistant to changes in temperature and salinity, and will provide more stable conditions for the 'ōpae 'ula. We recommend using containers that hold at least a quart of water. This will comfortably support about a half dozen 'ōpae 'ula. The container should have a tight fitting lid (nonmetallic) to minimize evaporation. A layer of beach sand about a half-inch to an inch deep should cover the bottom of the container. The calcium carbonate in the beach sand will help to buffer the water and help maintain a proper pH. This sand can be purchased from a local petshop. Decorative rocks and/or plastic aquarium plants should be added to provide shelter and additional surfaces for algae to grow.

'Ōpae 'ula can be found in anchialine pools with a wide range of salinities, which can change even on a daily basis with the rising and falling of the tides. These 'ōpae are therefore very adaptable. Based on our experience, we've found that a good salinity can be attained by mixing one part of seawater to 2 to 3 parts of freshwater. This will give you a salinity of 9 to 12 parts of salt to a thousand parts of water (ppt.). Freshwater is 0 ppt. and full strength seawater is 35 ppt. After filling your container with this water mixture, mark the water level with a Sharpie, and cover the container as best you can. When the water level drops due to evaporation, add freshwater to the same mark.

An important consideration is finding the right spot in your home or office for your micro-habitat. A good location would be somewhere that gets bright indirect light—near a window, or under a light. It should not receive direct sunlight or be placed too close to an incandescent bulb—both will overheat the micro-habitat and kill the 'ōpae 'ula.

Your micro-habitat should require very little maintenance. The 'ōpae 'ula will feed on the algae, so you will not need to add any additional food. Check the water level and replace the evaporated water as needed. If you notice 'ōpae 'ula carrying eggs, check your jar in about 3 to 4 weeks, and look for the larval 'ōpae 'ula. They will be swimming near the water's surface in a vertical position.

Biospheres and Micro-Habitats

Biology teacher, Kristen Ono, with future marine biologist, son Caleb, enjoying their 'opae 'ula biosphere.

If you ever tire of your micro-habitat, give it to a friend, donate it to a school, or return the 'ōpae 'ula to the petshop. Do not release the 'ōpae 'ula back into an anchialine pool. This may sound strange from a conservation standpoint, but as we explained in an earlier chapter, 'ōpae 'ula on the different islands, and even in different areas of the same island have evolved into distinct lineages. Releasing 'ōpae 'ula from a different lineage into an anchialine pool probably won't undo hundreds of years of evolution, but it may generate misleading data for scientists analyzing the DNA of the different populations of 'ōpae 'ula.

On a final note, it is our sincerest hope that *Hawaiian Anchialine Pools: Windows to a Hidden World* is a beginning toward a better understanding of the beauty and fragile nature of these pools and the unique creatures that live in them.

Mahalo for allowing us to share our journey with you!

—Mike, Tom and Annette

References

Anker, A. 2010. *Metabetaeus* Borradaile, 1899 revisited, with description of a new marine species from French Polynesia (Crustacea: Decapoda: Alpheidae). Zootaxa 2552: 37 - 54.

Bailey-Brock, J.H., V.R. Brock and R.E. Brock. 1999. Intrusion of Anchialine Species in the Marine Environment: the Appearance of an endemic Hawaiian Shrimp, *Halocaridina rubra*, on the South Shore of Oʻahu (Hawaiian Islands). Pacific Science. Vol. 53(4):367-369

Bailey-Brock, J. H. and R. E. Brock. 1993. Feeding, reproduction, and sense organs of the Hawaiian anchialine shrimp *Halocaridina rubra* (Atyidae). Pacif. Sci. 47(4):338-355.

Banner, A. H. and D. M. Banner. 1974. Contributions to the Knowledge of the Alpheid Shrimp of the pacific Ocean. Part XVII. Additional Notes on the Hawaiian Alpheids: New Species, Subspecies and Some Nomenclatorial Changes. Pacific Science. 28:423-437.

Banner, A. H. and D. M. Banner. 1960. Contributions to the Knowledge of the Alpheid Shrimp of the Pacific Ocean. Part VII. On *Metabetaeus* Borradaile, with a New Species from Hawaii. Pacific Science. 28: 299–303.

Bozanic, J. 2004. Lua O Palahemo Cave, Ka Lae, Hawaiʻi. Hawaiʻi Speleological Survey Newsletter. pg. 4-5.

Brock, R. E. and J. H. Brock. 2014. Personal communication. University of Hawaiʻi at Mānoa.

Brock, R. E. 2011. Water Quality and Anchialine Pool Monitoring in Support of the Development at Kukiʻo, North Kona, 2010 Annual Report. Environmental Assessment Co. EAC Report No. 2011-06.

Brock, R. E. 2004. Anchialine Resources in Two Hawaiʻi State Natural Area Reserves: ʻĀhihi-Kīnaʻu, Maui Island and Manukā, Hawaiʻi Island with Recommendations for their Management. Environmental Assessment, LLC. Honolulu. EAC Report No. 2004-15. 60 pp.

Brock, R.E. & J.H. Bailey-Brock. 1998. An unique anchialine pool in the Hawaiian Islands. Internat. Rev. Hydrobiol., 83:65-75.

Brock, R.E. & A. Kam. 1997. Biological and Water Quality Characteristics of Anchialine Resources in Kaloko-Honōkohau National Historical

Park. Cooperative National Park Resources Studies Unit, CA 8008-2-9004. Technical Report 112, pp. 1-110.

Brock, R.E. and J.H. Bailey-Brock. 1995. Anchialine resources of Kahoʻolawe, Hawaiʻi. In: An Evaluation of the Nearshore Coral Reef Resources of Kahoʻolawe, Hawaiʻi-June 1995. Coral Reef Assessment and Monitoring Program. 20p.

Brock, R. E. and A. Kam. 1994. The Waikoloa Anchialine Pond Program Fifth Status Report. Waikoloa Anchialine Pond Management Program. University of Hawaiʻi. HIMB/SeaGrant. 71 pp.

Brock, R. E. 1993. Second Semiannual Monitoring Report on the Anchialine Pool biota at Mauna Lani Resort, Inc., South Kohala, Hawaiʻi. Environmental Assessment Co. Honolulu. EAC Report No. 92-19.

Brock, R. E. 1987. Characteristics of Water Quality in Anchialine Ponds of the Kona Hawaiʻi Coast. Pacific Science. 41: 200-208

Brock, R.E. 1985. An assessment of the conditions and future of the anchialine pond resources of the Hawaiian Islands. Appendix C, pp. C-1-C-12. In: U.S. Army Corps of Engineers, Honolulu District. Final environmental Impact Statement US Department of the Army Permit Application, Waikoloa Beach Resort, Waikoloa, South Kohala District, Island of Hawaiʻi. September 1985.

Brock, R.E. 1977. Occurrence and Variety of Fishes in Mixohaline Ponds of the Kona, Hawaiʻi, Coast. Copeia. No. 1, pp. 134-139.

Bruce, A.J. 2005. *Palaemonella burnsi* Holthuis, 1973, a pontoniine shrimp (Crustacea: Decapoda: Palaemonicae) new to the Japanese fauna. Cahiers de Biologie Marine. 46:211-215.

Chace, F. Jr. & R.B. Manning. 1972. Two new Caridean shrimps, one representing a new family, from marine pools on Ascension Island (Crustacea: Decapoda:Natantia). Smithsonian Contributions to Zoology, No. 131, 18 pp.

Chai, D.K., L.W. Cuddihy and C.P. Stone. 1989. An Inventory and Assessment of Anchialine Pools in Hawaiʻi Volcanoes National Park From Wahaʻula to Kaʻaha, Puna and Kaʻū, Hawaiʻi. Cooperative National Park Resources Studies Unit. CA 8015-2-0001. Technical Report 69, pp. 37.

Clark, S.D., D. Gosser & R. Nees. 2004. Archaelogical Inventory Survey for the proposed Waiʻanae Regional Park, Waiʻanae Kai Ahupuaʻa,

O'ahu, Hawai'i TMK:8-5-02:11. Pacific Consulting Services Inc., 720 Iwilei Rd., Ste. 424, Honolulu, HI 96817, 75 pp.

Couret, C.L. Jr. and D.C.L. Wong. 1978. Larval development of *Halocaridina rubra* Holthuis (Decapoda, Atyidae). Crustaceana 34:301-309.

Craft, J.D., A.D. Russ, M.N. Yamamoto, T.Y. Iwai Jr., S. Hau, J. Kahiapo, C.T. Chong, S. Ziegler-Chong, C. Muir, Y. Fujita, D.A. Polhemus, R.A. Kinzie III, and S.R. Santos. 2008. Islands under islands: The phylogeography and evolution of *Halocaridina rubra* Holthuis, 1963 (Crustacean: Decapoda: Atyidae) in the Hawaiian archipelago. Limnol. Oceanogr., 53:675-689.

De Grave, S. and T.S. Sakihara. 2011. Further records of the anchialine shrimp, *Periclimenes pholeter* Holthius, 1973 (Crustacea, Dcapoda, Palaemonidae). Zootaxa 2903: 64-68.

FishBase. 2007. Froese, R. and D. Pauly (Eds) . World Wide Web electronic publication. http://www.fishbase.org (version 022/2007).

Donachie, S.P., S. Hou, K.S. Lee, C.W. Riley, A. Pikina, C. Belisle, S. Kempe, T.S. Gregory, A. Bossuyt, J. Boerema, J. Liu, T.A. Freitas, A. Malahoff and M. Alam. 2004. The Hawaiian Archipelago: A Microbial Diversity Hotspot. Microbial Ecology. 48(4):509-520.

Donachie, S.P., R.A. Kinzie III, R.R. Bidigare, D.W. Sadler, D.M. Karl. 1999. Lake Kauhakō, Moloka'i, Hawai'i: Biological and Chemical Aspects of a Morpho-Ectogenic Meromictic lake. Aquatic Microbial Ecology. Vol. 19: 93 – 103.

Fransen, C.H.J.M., S. De Grave and T.S. Sakihara. 2013. New records of *Vetericaris chaceorum* (Decapoda, Procarididae) From Hawai'i. Crustaceana 86(5) 625-631.

Halliday, W.R. 1997. Current Status of the 'Ewa Karst, Honolulu County, Hawai'i. World Wide Web electronic Publication. www.caves.org/section/ccms/wrh/.

Havird, J. C., S. R. Santos and R. P. Henry. 2014. Osmoregulation in the Hawaiian anchialine shrimp *Halocaridina rubra* (Crustacea: Atyidae): Expression of Ion Transporters, Mitochondria-rich cell Proliferation and Hemolymph Osmolality During Saline Transfers. J Exp Biol Advance Online Articles. 47 pp.

Hawai'i Heritage Program and The Nature Conservancy of Hawai'i. 1987. Biological database of rare species and natural communities in anchialine ponds of the State of Hawai'i. Prepared for the County of Hawai'i, 50pp.

Holthuis, L.B. 1963. On red colourerd shrimps (Decapoda, Caridea) from tropical land-locked saltwater pools. Zoologische Mededelingen, 33(16):261-279.

Holthuis, L.B. 1973. Caridean shrimps found in land-locked saltwater pools at four Indo-West Pacific localities (Sinai Peninsula, Funafuti Atoll, Maui and Hawai'i Islands), with a description of one new genus and four new species. Zool. Verhand. 128:1- 48.

Hoover, J.P. 1999. Hawai'i's Sea Creatures, A Guide to Hawai'i's Marine Invertebrates. Mutual Publishing. Honolulu. 366 pp.

Ivey, J. & S.R. Santos. 2007. The complete mitochondrial genome of the Hawaiian anchialine shrimp *Halocaridina rubra* Holthuis, 1963 (Crustacea: Decapoda: Atyidae). J. Gene, 394:35-44.

Iwai Jr., T. 2005. Captive Breeding of the endemic Hawaiian red shrimp, *Halocaridina rubra*. Part 1: Reproduction, larvae development, and first feeding. Presentation at the 2005 Hawai'i Conservation conference—"Hawai'i's Restoration Efforts". Division of Aquatic Resources, Ānuenue Fisheries Research Center, 1039 Sand Island Parkway, Honolulu, HI 96819. 24 pp.

Kahiapo, J.N. 2010. Personal communication. State of Hawai'i, Department of Land and Natural Resources, Division of Aquatic Resources

Kensley, B. and D. Williams. 1986. New shrimps (Families Procarididae and Atyidae) from a submerged lava tube on Hawai'i. Jour. Crustacean Biol. 6:417-437.

Liu, M. Y., Y. X. Cai and C. S. Tzeng. 2007. Molecular Systematics of the Freshwater Prawn Genus *Macrobrachium* Bate, 1868 (Crustacea: Decapoda: Palaemonidae) Inferred from mtDNA Sequences, with Emphasis on East Asian Species. Zoological Studies 46(3):272-289.

Maciolek, J. 1986. Environmental features and biota of anchialine pools on Cape Kina'u, Maui, Hawai'i. Stygologia, 2:119-129.

Maciolek, J.A. 1983. Distribution and biology of Indo-Pacific insular hypogeal shrimps. Bull. Mar. Sci., 33:606-618.

Maciolek, J.A. 1982. Lake and Lake-like Waters of the Hawaiian Archipelago. Occasional Papers of Bernice P. Bishop Museum. 25: 1-14.

References

Maciolek, J.A. & R.E. Brock. 1974. Aquatic Survey of the Kona Coast Ponds, Hawai'i Island. Sea Grant Advisory Report, UNIHI-SEAGRANT-AR-74-04. 73 pp.

Marizot, D.C.; M.E. Schmidt; and M.P. Weinstein. 1993. Genetic variabilitiy in two anchialine shrimps in the Hawaiian Islands. KEMRON Environmental Services, Inc., 33 Walt Whitman Rd., Huntington Station, New York, 11746. 21 pp.

Meredith, J. S. and W. D. Williams. 1981. The Occurrence of *Antecaridina lauensis* (Edmonson) (Crustacea, Decapoda, Atyidae) in the Solomon Islands. Hydrobiologia. 85: 49 – 58.

National Park Service, U. S. Department of the Interior. 2010. Assessment of Natural Resources and Watershed Conditions for Kalaupapa National Historic Park. Natural Resources Report NPS/NPRC/WRD/NRR-2010/261.

Ng, P.K.L. 2011. *Pele ramseyi*, a new genus and species of anchialine swimming crab (Crustacea: Brachyura: Portunidae) from the Hawaiian Islands. Zootaxa 2737: 34-48.

Oceanic Institute, Inc. & D. Ziemann. 1985. Anchialine Pond Survey of the Northwest Coast of Hawai'i Island. Belt, Collins & Associates, 600 Coral Street, Honolulu, Hawai'i 96813. 62 pp.

Ridgley, M. & D.K. Chai. 1990. Evaluating potential biotic benefits from conservation: anchialine ponds in Hawai'i. The Environmental Professional, 12:214-228.

Russ, A., S.R. Santos, & C. Muir. 2010. Genetic population structure of an anchialine shrimp, *Metabetaeus lohena* (Crustacea:Alpheidae), in the Hawaiian Islands. Rev. Biol. Trop. (Int. J. Trop. Biol. ISSN-0034-7744), 58(1):159-170.

Sakihara, T. S. 2009. Mapping and inventory of Anchialine Pool Habitat and Biota in the Manukā Watershed and Natural Area Reserve, October 2008 to March 2009. Division of Aquatic Resources, Department of Land and Natural Resources, State of Hawai'i. DAR Technical Report 09-01. 35 pp.

Santos, S. R. and D. A. Weese. 2011. Rocks and clocks: linking geologic history and rates of genetic differentiation in anchialine organisms. Hydrobiologia, 677:53-64.

Santos, S.R. 2006. Patterns of genetic connectivity among anchialine habitats: a case study of the endemic Hawaiian shrimp *Halocaridina rubra* on the Island of Hawai'i. Mol. Ecol. 15:2699-2718.

The Nature Conservancy of Hawai'i. 1992. Biological database and reconnaissance survey of Kaho'olawe Island Conveyance Commission, Consultant Report 6.

Titcomb, M. 1978. Native Use of Marine Invertebrates in Old Hawai'i. Pacific Science, Vol. 32, no. 4

Vaught, R. C., J. C. Havird and S. R. Santos. 2014. Genetic Lineage and Environmental Conditions as Drivers of Chromatosome Variation in the Anchialine Shrimp *Halocaridina rubra* Holthuis, 1963 (Caridea: Atyidae). Journal of Crustacean Biology. Vol. 34, Issue 5, pp. 647 – 657.

Williamson, D. I. 1969. Names of larvae in the Decapoda and Euphausiacea. Crustaceana, 16(2):210-213.

Wong, D. 1975. Algae of the anchialine pools at Cape Kina'u, Maui, and aspects of the trophic ecology of *Halocardina rubra* Holthuis (Decapoda, Atyidae). M.S. thesis, University of Hawai'i at Mānoa, Honolulu.103 pp.

Yamamoto, M.N. and A.W. Tagawa. 2000. Hawai'i's Native & Exotic Freshwater Animals. Mutual Publishing. Honolulu. 200 pp.

Ziemann, D. A. 1988. Impact analysis for construction of Recreational Marina of Kohanaiki, Island of Hawai'i. Engineering Concepts, Inc. Honolulu. 31 pp.

Index

A

Abudefuf abdominalis (see also Mamo), 59
'Āhihi-Kīna'u Natural Area Reserve, 5-7, 17, 38, 45-47, 81, 88
Āholehole (see also *Kuhlia sandvicensis*, *Kuhlia xenura*), 51, 58-60
'Akulikuli-kai (see also *Batis maritima*), 51
Allen Davis Beach, O'ahu, 59-60
Amphidromy, 53, 64
'Anaeho'omalu, Hawai'i, 3
Angelfish (see also Cichlidae), 62
Antecaridina lauensis, 17, 32-34, 43, 68-69
Atya bisulcata (see also 'Ōpae kala'ole), 54
Awaous stamineus (see also 'O'opu nākea), 55

B

B6-139 sinkhole, 76-80
Barbers Point Harbor/Naval Air Station, 76-80, 89
Batis maritima (see also 'Akulikuli-kai), 51
Biospheres (see also Micro-habitats), 83-84, 96-99

C

Calliasmata pholidota, 3, 17, 31-32, 43, 46, 68
Campbell Industrial Park, O'ahu, 9, 89
Cichlidae (see also Angelfish, Tilapia, and Tucunare), 62-63
Clean Water Act, 85, 87
Corixidae (see also Water boatmen), 12
Cyanobacteria, 10, 67

D

Decapterus spp. (see also 'Ōpelu), 25
Disjunct distribution pattern, 32, 43, 68-69
DNA research, 60, 69-74, 96

E

Eleotris sandwicensis (see also 'O'opu 'akupa), 55-56
Epigeal, 2, 25, 75
'Ewa Plain, O'ahu, 8, 63, 76

F

Four Seasons Resort at Hualālai, Hawai'i, 86

G

Grapsus crabs, 46
Guppies (see also Topminnows, *Poecilia reticulata*), 62, 81-82, 88
Gymnothorax hilonis (see also Moray eel, Peppered moray, Puhi kāp'ā, *Gymnothorax pictus*), 58
Gymnothorax pictus (see also Moray eel, Peppered moray, Puhi kāp'ā, *Gymnothorax hilonis*), 58, 60

H

Hā'ena Wet Cave, Kaua'i, 12
Halocaridina palahemo, 22, 69
Halocaridina rubra (see also 'Ōpae 'ula), 3, 5, 17, 19, 34, 69, 78
Hawai'i Volcanoes National Park, 93-94
Hypogeal, 2, 24-25, 37, 69, 81

I

'Iolani Barracks, O'ahu, 8
'Iolani Palace, O'ahu, 8
Isaac Hale Beach Park, Hawai'i, 4

Index

K

Kahuku, Oʻahu, 13
Kalaeloa Unit, Pearl Harbor National Wildlife Refuge, 71, 89-95
Kalaupapa, Molokaʻi, 10
Kapapa Island, Oʻahu, 70
Kapolei, Oʻahu, 76
Karst, 8
Kauhakō Crater, Lake, Molokaʻi, 10
Kawaiahaʻo Church, Oʻahu, 8
Kiomoʻomo, 56
Kona Coast, Hawaiʻi, 3, 17, 51, 54, 70, 76, 83
Kuhlia sandvicensis (see also Āholehole, *Kuhlia xenura*), 60
Kuhlia xenura (see also Āholehole, *Kuhlia sandvicensis*), 60
Kūpīpī (*Abudefduf abdominalis*), 58

L

Lāwalu (cooking style), 56
Lecithotrophic larvae, 22, 72
Liberty mollies (see also Topminnows, *Poecilia* spp.), 62
Lua O Palahemo, Hawaiʻi, 3, 4, 22, 40-42, 69

M

Macrobrachium grandimanus (see also ʻŌpae ʻOehaʻa), 52
Macrobrachium lar (see also Tahitian prawn), 53, 63-64
Macrobrachium rosenbergii (see also Malaysian Prawn), 53
Malaysian prawn (see also *Macrobrachium rosenbergii*), 53
Mamo (see also *Abudefduf abdominalis*), 58-59
Manini (*Acanthurus triostegus*), 58
Manukā and Manukā Natural Area Reserve, 3-4, 17, 40-44
Menpachi (*Myripristis* spp.) (see also ʻūʻū), 59-60

Metabetaeus lohena, 5, 17, 26-30, 31-32, 43, 46, 68, 72-74, 80, 94
Micro-habitats (see also Biospheres), 24, 72, 83-84, 96-99
Molly (see also *Poecilia* spp., Poeciliidae), 62
Moonfish (see also Poeciliidae), 62
Moray eel (see also Peppered moray, Puhi kāpʻā, *Gymnothorax hilonis*, *Gymnothorax pictus*), 15, 58-59

N

Nuʻuanu Stream, Oʻahu, 64

O

ʻOama (*Mulloidichthys* spp.), 51
ʻOʻopu ʻakupa (see also *Eleotris sandwicensis*), 55-56
ʻOʻopu nākea, (see also *Awaous stamineus*), 55
ʻŌpae hiki (see also ʻŌpae ʻula, *Halocardina rubra*), 19
ʻŌpae huna (see also *Palaemon debilis*), 50-52
ʻŌpae kalaʻole (see also *Atya bisulcata*), 54
ʻŌpae ʻoehaʻa (see also *Macrobrachium grandimanus*), 52-54
ʻŌpae ʻula (see also ʻŌpae hiki, *Halocardina rubra*), 3, 5, 7, 10-16, 19-30, 31, 33-34, 38, 40, 47, 59-60, 63, 66, 69, 70-76, 78, 80-84, 88-89, 91-92, 94-99
ʻŌpelu (see also *Decapterus* spp.), 25

P

Palaemon debilis (see also ʻŌpae huna), 46, 50-52
Palaemonella burnsi, 17, 37-39, 52
Palu, 25
Papahānaumokuākea Marine National Monument, 14
Pāpio (*Caranx* spp., *Carangoides* spp.,

Index

Gnathanodon speciosus), 51, 56
Parhippolyte mistica, 47
Paspalum vaginatum (see also Seashore paspalum), 81
Peppered moray (see also Moray eel, Puhi kāpʻā, *Gymnothorax hilonis*, *Gymnothorax pictus*), 58
Pele ramseyi, 17, 45-48
Pelekunu Stream, Molokaʻi, 64
Periclimenes pholeter, 17, 43-44
Planktotrophic larvae, 29, 73
Poecilia reticulata (see also Guppies, Topminnows, Poeciliidae), 81-82, 88
Poecilia spp. (see also Liberty mollies, Topminnows), 62
Poeciliidae (see also Guppies, Molly, Moonfish, Topminnows, *Poecilia reticulata*, *Poecilia* spp.), 62
Pohoiki Hot Springs, Hawaiʻi, 4-5
Procarididae, 36, 41
Procaris hawaiana, 3, 17, 35-36, 41, 46
Puʻu Lohena, Hawaiʻi, 30
Puhi kāpʻā (see also Moray eel, Peppered moray, *Gymnothorax hilonis*, *Gymnothorax pictus*), 58-59
Puna, 4

R

Rift zones, 74
Rotenone, 87
Ruppia maritima (see also Widgeon grass), 66

S

Sailors Hat, Kahoʻolawe, 1, 11-13
Sarotherodon melanotheron (see also Tilapia, Black-Chin), 62-63
Seashore paspalum (see also *Paspalum vaginatum*), 81-83
South Point, Hawaiʻi, 3, 30, 40
Stalactites, 76, 79

Swordtail (see also Poeciliidae), 62

T

Tahitian prawn (see also *Macrobrachium lar*), 53, 62-64
Tilapia, Black-Chin (see also *Sarotherodon melanotheron*), 62-64, 81
Topminnows (see also Guppies, Liberty mollies, Molly, *Poecilia reticulata*, *Poecilia* spp., Poeciliidae), 62-64, 81
Tucunare (see also Cichlidae), 62

U

ʻŪʻū (see also menpachi), 59

V

Vetericaris chaceorum, 3-4, 17, 40-44

W

Waiʻanae, Oʻahu, 8, 77
Waikoloa Beach Marriot Resort and Spa, Hawaiʻi, 85
Waiʻānapanapa Cave, Maui, 6-7, 81-82, 88
Water boatmen (see also Corixidae), 12
Widgeon grass (see also *Ruppia maritima*), 66

About the Authors

Mike N. Yamamoto was born and raised in Honolulu, Hawai'i. He attended Mānoa Elementary School, Robert Louis Stevenson Intermediate School, Roosevelt High School, and the University of Hawai'i at Mānoa, where he earned a Bachelor's and Master's degree in Zoology. He began his career as an Aquatic Biologist with the Division of Aquatic Resources (formerly Division of Fish and Game) in 1976, and retired in 2008.

As a child, Mike remembers spending all of his spare time exploring neighborhood streams, and accompanying his family on countless camping trips to the seashore at Hale'iwa, Makapu'u and Ka'ena Point. His interest in biology and becoming a marine biologist was sparked by all of the fascinating discoveries made during these outings. Mike credits his parents, Miye and George Yamamoto, and his wife Karen for supporting him in all of his endeavors. He was also fortunate to have two exceptional teachers, who encouraged and inspired him: Karen Muronaka, his Biology/Zoology teacher at Roosevelt High School, and Dr. Fred Kamemoto, his mentor at the University of Hawai'i. Finally, Mike is grateful for his good friends and co-workers: Thomas Iwai Jr., Annette Tagawa and Lorraine Takaoka, who made working at the Division of Aquatic Resources an enjoyable experience.

Thomas Y. Iwai Jr. was born and raised in Honolulu, Hawai'i and attended Kalihi-Waena Elementary School, Kalākaua Intermediate School, Wallace Rider Farrington High School, and the University of Hawai'i at Mānoa where he earned a Bachelor of Arts degree in Zoology and a Master's degree in Animal Sciences (Aquaculture Nutrition). He began his career in 1973 at the Ānuenue Fisheries Research Center (AFRC), Division of Aquatic Resources, as a volunteer student involved with the larval rearing and growout culture of the giant Malaysian prawn *(Macrobrachium rosenbergii)*. After graduating from the UH, he was hired as a full time Aquatic Biologist conducting research at the AFRC on the development of other potential aquatic species for Hawai'i's fledgling aquaculture industry.

Tom's love for the ocean began at an early age growing up in Kalihi with frequent trips to the beach with family and friends. Although fishing was always fun, investigating the tidepools and their strange inhabitants, capturing them and studying them in captivity became a favorite past time. His inquisitiveness as to how the 'ōpae 'ula were able to survive and reproduce in a seemingly "hostile" anchialine environment led to the collaborative effort with the other authors. Tom credits his hardworking parents, Thomas and Doris Iwai who always emphasized the importance of doing your best and getting a good education, and to his wife, Sharon for supporting his home experiments and endeavors, however "crazy" they may seem. Special thanks also to Takuji Fujimura, for being a mentor and dear friend who always emphasized that "Fear of failure should never stop anyone from doing their best and what's right."

Finally, to my major 'ōpae 'ula competitor, Mike Yamamoto, who constantly tested our individual ingenuity and creativity and to Annette Tagawa, the 'soul' behind this book, whose patience, persistence, and perseverence made the completion of this book possible. A big Mahalo to both of them for their support, encouragement and friendship.

Annette W. Tagawa, formerly Annette W. Young, was born and raised in Honolulu, Hawai'i. She attended Likelike Elementary School, St. Theresa's School, Maryknoll High School and the University of Hawai'i at Mānoa where she earned a Bachelor's degree in Zoology. She began working as a Fishery Aid for the Division of Aquatic Resources in 1981 and is currently an Aquatic Biologist for the Division. Her interest in anchialine pool ecosystems grew with the exciting opportunity to work on this Division project with her exceptional colleagues, mentors and co-authors, Mike Yamamoto and Thomas Iwai Jr.

Annette's interest in marine biology began in high school with volunteer opportunities at the Waikīkī Aquarium helping to teach children about marine life in Hawai'i. She credits her family for inspiring her love for the outdoors and Leslie K. Matsuura, formally of the Waikīkī

Aquarium, for being a mentor and inspiring her love for the marine environment and for the memory of her very first glimpse of an ʻōpae ʻula gracefully swimming in a glass jar biosphere on his office desk. Most of all, she would like to thank her co-workers Mike Yamamoto and Thomas Iwai Jr. for all their friendship and support throughout the years.